OFF-LOOM WEAVING

Hand-woven patterns and inspiration

OFF-LOOM WEAVING

Hand-woven patterns and inspiration

SARAH WARD PODLEŚNY

HERBERT PRESS
LONDON • OXFORD • NEW YORK • NEW DELHI • SYDNEY

HERBERT PRESS
Bloomsbury Publishing Plc
50 Bedford Square, London, WC1B 3DP, UK
Bloomsbury Publishing Ireland Limited
29 Earlsfort Terrace, Dublin 2, D02 AY28, Ireland

BLOOMSBURY, HERBERT PRESS and the Herbert Press logo
are trademarks of Bloomsbury Publishing Plc

First published in Great Britain in 2026

A catalogue record for this book is available from the British Library
Library of Congress Cataloguing-in-Publication data has been applied for

ISBN: 978-1-78994-362-7; eBook: 978-1-78994-361-0

2 4 6 8 10 9 7 5 3 1

Typeset and designed by Tina Hobson
Printed and bound in Italy by L.E.G.O.

FSC www.fsc.org MIX Paper | Supporting responsible forestry FSC® C023419

To find out more about our authors and books visit www.bloomsbury.com and
sign up for our newsletters
For product safety related questions contact productsafety@bloomsbury.com

Contents

Introduction

My Journey into Off-loom Weaving

My first encounter in the 'weave room' at university was a sensory experience. I don't remember my first warp, but I do remember the smell of the studio, the rhythmic crashing sounds of the huge wooden floor looms, the kindness of our tutor. Shuttles whizzing across warps, pedals being worked, the old pegs and lags rotating around the inner mechanism of the looms. Everyone was deep in the zone, lost in the flow of process, each hammering out their own individual stories through the interlacing of colour, texture and structure.

I've been a weaver for fifteen years now – mostly working with a variety of big, beautiful wooden floor looms. When Covid hit, for the first time in years I couldn't just go to the studio and weave. I got on with other useful things – research, planning, life admin – but after a while, I found that I just wanted to weave something. I was so used to toiling away at the loom every day, playing with yarn, colour and textures. I missed working with my hands, exploring ideas and translating them into tangible forms. Weaving had become a daily therapy, offering moments of calm, a sense of progress and that satisfying feeling of having made something from scratch. The tools and threads that were so familiar in my hands had represented a wellspring of possibilities that now felt strangely out of reach.

The limitations imposed during lockdown presented a challenge: how could I find ways of weaving without my loom, using only what I had available within the confines of my home? I found a small spool of dark blue cotton in a drawer, located a needle from a hotel sewing kit and used little pieces of cardboard from an old box to make small studies of my favourite woven structures: twill, herringbone, hopsack and houndstooth. Before long, I started to weave around blocks of wood, rocks, slate and any other found objects I could get my hands on.

▲ The Weave Workshop at Central Saint Martins, UAL (photo: Philippa Brock)

Eventually, I regained access to my studio, but I found that rather than feeling drawn back to my looms I was more enticed by my yarn stash. I rediscovered numerous types of thread in my studio that day: soft cotton; textural linen; hairy wool; shining silk; a variety of weights from my denim-weaving days, ecru and white; a box of sewing thread; some flat gima cotton from Japan; a bag of embroidery floss bursting with colour; an irregular slub; a stiff cotton cord; and some chunky balls of rug wool inherited from a local guild member. These were all left over from my days as a design studio, now presenting themselves for use in a different way.

As I explored this new-found technique further, I discovered that it was possible to create fabrics that were similar to those woven on a 'proper' loom. However, presented as 'woven wrappings' around a simple four-sided base, they felt more like artworks to me. Relieved of the burden of functionality, they became a celebration of iconic and historic woven fabrics, of fibre, and of woven structure as an art form in its own right.

Weaving slowly has made space for more thoughtful observation. Taking the process of weaving back to the basics of hand and material also helped me to gain a deeper appreciation for the skill and craftsmanship of our predecessors.

I found myself teleported back through time, the movements of my fingers mirroring those of the many weavers who came before me. Knowledge that the materials and methods of weaving have remained relatively unchanged for millennia conjures a strong connection between past and present. These small explorations are therapeutic, mindful. Their potential as an educational tool became clear when I realised that by weaving this way, it was possible to gain a better understanding of the very structures I had taken for granted at the loom for many years.

During lockdown, the challenge of working within limitations sparked ideas that would have been unlikely to surface were all of my usual options available to me. Regaining access to my studio confronted me with the amount of yarn I had accumulated over the years and hadn't used. As I sorted through my collection, I started to think about the many 'uses' of thread, pondering not only its role as a fibre for textile making but as a vehicle for learning about history and culture. When we learn about a type of textile, we are offered a glimpse through a window into another time. Through the development of fibre, fabric and dyes, we can trace the lives of people and communities, both through the stories they shared as they passed their skills down and the ways the cloth itself changed as production methods continue to evolve.

Of the five looms that once inhabited my studio, just one remains now – an old WeaveMaster that my dad, Henryk, and I restored together. With its beautifully carved wooden cranks and solid build, it feels sturdier than some modern looms. I bought it from someone in Surrey who'd had it in her attic for forty years. She shared that it was handmade and originally used by World War II veterans, not just for work but also as a form of therapy and rehabilitation. The concept of weaving as occupational therapy is of great interest to me. Over the years, it has become apparent to me that throughout history, craft has repeatedly shown up for us in our time of need – and not just for its practical uses.

How To Use This Book

This is a book about weaving, but it's also about community, storytelling, well-being and the value of craft. I hope to offer relatability and to reinforce the idea that time spent making things is time well spent. As part of my research, I asked my own creative community to share their craft experiences with me. Insights into those can be found sprinkled throughout the book, along with my own. As a teacher, I have many moments of 'me too!' when talking with participants about our thoughts and experiences on making, but what I find even more interesting are all the ways in which we differ. Although there are many aspects of craft and creativity that we can relate on, we don't all experience it the same way – we all have our own unique relationship to making. We've all arrived here from different starting points, but we're here and that's what matters.

There are eleven how-to projects in this book for you to try. We'll start simple with paper weaving, and then we'll move on to using needle and thread to weave around a variety of bases. First I'll show you some simple structures like twill and hopsack, which can be used to make lots of different patterns including dogtooth and checks, and later I'll teach you how to create a three-dimensional pattern called waffle. It's easy once you know how. All you really need to learn is one simple structure, and then – with the addition of colour and stripe – all sorts of discoveries can be made.

Through these pages, I will share with you my small corner of the weaving world and the immense joy and peace that it has brought me over the years. The first big challenge is starting; after that, the hardest thing is stopping!

Chapter 1

What is Off-loom Weaving?

Recently, a participant of one of my workshops told me she'd been out somewhere for the day and had taken her weaving with her. A stranger came over and asked her what she was doing. She excitedly told them: 'it's magic!' In my opinion, her words describe this craft perfectly.

Essentially, 'off-loom weaving' means weaving without a conventional loom – without shafts, heddles, levers, pedals or shuttles. There are many types of off-loom weaving: basket weaving, pin loom weaving, frame weaving, paper weaving, branch weaving, back strap weaving, rag rug weaving... even darning! Often, it means using whatever we have to hand and finding a way.

I am going to teach you how to weave around a solid base or found object, using needle and thread. Bridging the gap between simple frame weaving and 'proper' loom weaving, this iteration of 'off-loom' weaving will teach you the basics of woven cloth and construction without the added complexity of the loom to contend with. And the best part? It's portable! Unlike a big old solid loom, you can pop it in your bag and take it with you for a bit of 'al fresco' crafting; to the beach, out in the garden, on the bus, or just on the sofa (my all-time favourite). This type of weaving is suitable for total beginners and seasoned weavers alike, and can be enjoyed by all age groups from children of around eight years old upwards. If you're thinking of learning how to weave on a loom, small-scale off-loom weaving projects are a great way to 'dip your feet' before taking the plunge.

Using needle and thread slows down the weaving process and engages us more fully with each 'over and under' in a way that doesn't happen in such clear focus at the loom. The up-close view of the process helps us to understand the basic logic of fabric construction. Weaving with needle and thread breaks the process down to simply warp and weft, under and over. It's also great fun as a stand-alone craft and has plenty of mileage by itself – these little woven studies make lovely gifts and beautiful artworks for the wall. In terms of pattern, the possibilities are endless.

From the perspective of a loom weaver, this is the perfect tool for testing out warp stripes, palettes and structures before committing to longer lengths at the loom. Compared to setting up for loom weaving, this warp-making process is quick and can really help during the planning stage. Small-scale weaving projects only require small amounts of yarn, and this technique offers a great solution for all your leftover scraps from other projects. Even the smallest amount can be put to good use, and there is a beauty in the spontaneity of choosing only from what you have available.

This particular type of off-loom weaving involves wrapping 'warp' threads longways around a base, and then weaving 'weft' threads in horizontally with a needle. After each woven row, the remaining thread is wrapped around the back, and all the way around to the front to begin the next row. Instead of weaving back and forth as in frame weaving, each row begins from the same side.

The 'wrapping' of threads around a solid base means that the threads themselves can be more densely packed without gaps between, and also removes the risk of warp threads 'pulling in' at the edges during the weaving process. This technique makes it possible to produce a wider range of structures and patterns, so that we might replicate fabrics that are closer to those woven on an actual loom or that you might recognise from the clothes in your wardrobe.

Artists' Examples

There are so many different types of off-loom weaving that exist, besides my iteration of it. Here's a small collection of some other artists' works.

▲ *After The Fall*, Clare Dudeney

▲ *Hybrid Objects*, Alice Fox

Clare Dudeney's intricate works resemble magnified swatches with looping, entwined threads and delicately trailing colour-glazed strands. Hard surfaces hold the memory of soft gestures. The extruded clay, formed into hollow hexagonal tubes, carries an industrial character that becomes supple through the weaving process. To fit the kiln shelf, the piece is split in two – a clean divide that becomes a feature. Once bisque-fired, the surface is meticulously painted with brush-on earthenware glazes, exploring texture and contrast: sandy and rusty browns, muted tertiaries, set against vivid pink, peach and mustard yellow.

Hybrid Objects forms part of a series exploring old tools and other materials found on Alice Fox's allotment plot. The majority of Alice's work is focused around using materials from the plot – found objects combined with cultivated and wild plants. Taking a playful approach to a set of old tools led her to explore ways she could bring different materials together. This resulted in forms that suggest function but are essentially sculptural.

▲ *Chromatic Connections*, Amber Roper of The Blühen Studio

▲ *Dead Mother Series*, Philippa Brock

▲ *Shoulder Boulder*, Rachael Matthews (photo Antranig Basman)

Amber Roper's 100 × 100 × 4cm (39 × 39 × 1½in) work carries a strong sense of connection and resilience through weaving. Using a variety of materials, textures and colourful woven structures, including polyester, wool, wire, cotton, cord, ribbon yarn, wood, water-based paints and copper pipes, this piece invites the viewer to experience collaboration – different elements uniting to form a single, harmonious whole.

Dead Mother Series takes a material memory approach from a seventy-year-old domestic collection of remnants and meterage of used and unused textiles that were intended for dressmaking/interiors projects. This series was an opportunity to explore the collected fabrics of Philippa Brock's late mother, and explores ideas around patchwork, which traditionally reuses and recycles textile scraps. The initial works use a recurring motif of striped textiles, the process involving cutting the fabric into strips, hand weaving, and stitching onto newsprint to stabilise their woven structure.

Shoulder Boulder features on the front cover of *Rag Manifesto* – a book by artist and rag rug weaver, Rachael Matthews. It is made from textile factory waste, woven on hand-built looms made by the artist out of scrap wood. The looms were made in irregular shapes to create a polyhedral sphere. The piece is part of a series of rag boulders, made in response to the overwhelming amount of textile waste strewn across the planet. The boulders are made as a storage solution for treasured textiles that travel through life with us, and hold special stories that need to be told.

Chapter 2

Community

Have you ever noticed how intertwined 'textiles' and 'storytelling' are in our spoken language? After all, weaving was always something that was done together – and humans are massive gossips. Though sometimes thought of as a negative trait, 'gossip' actually played an important role in social bonding for early humans, which was key to our survival.

The connection is evident in everyday phrases such as spinning a yarn (telling a lie); the unpicking or unravelling of a mystery; the fabric of life; weaving something into the narrative; the unfolding of a story; following the thread of a tale; a fabrication or embellishment of the truth; a tight-knit community. If you are on tenterhooks (the name of a frame used for stretching fabric to a high tension for drying), you feel tense with anticipation. The term pulling at a thread to see what comes loose brings to mind the feeling of having a dizzying hunch but being slightly afraid of what we might uncover. This language speaks to a long history of communal crafting, and of the important role that storytelling has played in creating a harmonious and productive workforce.

In *Resilient Stitch*, Claire Wellesley-Smith speaks about studying old textiles, of the way threadbare areas and patches of darning or stitch work 'add a layer of narrative', offering clues as to how the owner of the textile lived and how important it was for them to preserve their clothing. I often wonder about their stories, what their daily lives might have looked like. Like us, textiles can be moulded, manipulated, fall apart, be repaired, be changed. They hold memories and scars – the traces of their makers – and can provide warmth and comfort for others.

Looking Back to Look Forward

Throughout history, the discovery of human-made objects and textiles has helped us to construct our timeline, providing new insights as well as supporting already established theories.

Thanks to the preserving nature of burial rituals, ancient textiles have provided us with a great deal of knowledge about civilisations that came before us. Motifs, colour and patterns can indicate things like social status and beliefs and values. These artefacts offer us clues about the skill sets, techniques and methods of their craftspeople. Under the microscope, we can determine which plants might have been cultivated for use as fibre and dyestuff, and in turn what kinds of jobs they may have provided. In place of written documentation long perished, these textiles play an integral role in helping us to piece together our history; they tell a story about us.

Place

Fabrics have a deep connection to place. Each type of woven cloth offers us a story about its makers and the cultures they had sprung from. Some woven cloths are named after the region from which they originated; calico from Calicut, cashmere from Kashmir, the Madras check, the dungaree from Dongri, denim from Nimes and worsted wool from Worstead, Norfolk.

Some fabrics known to us in the West are referred to not by place of origin, but, slightly misleadingly, by the place in which they were first encountered by Europeans along the trade routes. For example, though first produced in Dhaka, Bangladesh, muslin became known as such after it was traded in Mosul, Iraq. Similarly, paisley, which has origins in India and Iran and was originally known as 'boteh' or 'buta', was later produced with great success in the town of Paisley in Scotland, from where it now takes its name.

Today, these fabrics are produced all over the world, as part of a huge global industry. Now so widely available, it is easy to forget these origin stories, along with the people, the labour, the skills behind the cloth. The farmers, the spinners, the dyers, the weavers, the fullers, the finishers, the stitchers. Many hands were and are involved in the making of cloth.

It Takes a Village

Until the industrial revolution, communities would work together using time-honoured skills passed down from generation to generation to produce useful items of wood, metal, clay, leather or textile. Often referred to as 'folk craft' or 'cottage industries', families or groups of families and locals would participate in small-scale production at home or in communal spaces.

The various processes involved in fabric production were mostly done by women. Stories were shared and songs were sung to pass the time and to make the work more enjoyable. Songs were usually built around the repetitive, rhythmic elements of the work. The Scottish folk tradition of 'waulking' or 'fulling' the fabric was one such task, involving soaking and beating the woven cloth to produce a softer finish. Women would gather around a table, passing sections of the fabric down the line, rhythmically beating it as they went, and singing their songs. The songs typically took the form of 'call and answer', with one singing a line then the group in unison singing it back, or in answer. Often, the lyrics described nature, animals and place, with humour sprinkled in here and there and ad-lib verses about local people, romances and scandalous goings-on.

In eighteenth-century Germany, spinning rooms would have been important social epicentres. In fact, the spinning room was one of the few places men and women could freely mingle, outside of the church. The term 'spinster', though originally simply meaning 'female spinner' holds a well-known connection to courtship. Travellers and journeymen were welcomed into these communal spaces to tell of their adventures and of life outside of the village.

Back in 2023 I visited my local Guild of Weavers, Spinners & Dyers. As I stepped into the room, I felt I had travelled back in time. A room full of traditional spinning wheels of all shapes and sizes, positioned in a circle. All wooden, all moving rhythmically, accompanied by the gentle chatter of the women wielding them. Some were learning, some were teaching. Their hands were well acquainted with their materials, moving almost independently of their owners, their actions as familiar as breathing.

▲ The Mid Essex Guild of Weavers, Spinners & Dyers

The Fabric of Society

Written references to the strong link between craft and community can be found at least as far back as the Ancient Greeks. In his work, *The Statesman*, Plato explores the topic of leadership and how best to maintain a harmonious and functional society with democracy and social justice at its heart.

Presented as a fictional dialogue between characters, weaving terms are used to describe 'unity' as the key component for success; individual threads representing a diversity of people, classes, ideas and perspectives, woven together with skill into the fabric of society. This 'kingly art' is described by a character called The Stranger: '...the whole process of royal weaving is comprised – never to allow temperate natures to be separated from the brave, but to weave them together, like the warp and the woof'. In his later work, *The Laws*, Plato uses this metaphor again, speaking of warp as strength and weft as softness, when describing the coming together of a diverse people, their differences an asset.

It was partly the development of handcrafts and skills that brought early humans together, out of nomadic isolation and into the first community settlements. The sharing of skills and collaborative work forged bonds and made us more resilient.

Skills, knowledge and techniques passed down over millennia have been integral to the development of today's textile industry. The intricate mechanisms of machines that now produce most of our everyday items are based on techniques developed by human hands. And, though often not acknowledged or fairly compensated for, human hands still play an integral role at every stage of production.

Since the industrial revolution, speed, profit and convenience have taken precedent above quality, craftsmanship and ethics. In many aspects of life today, it could be said that we have lost our sense of community spirit and collaboration, but it is alive and well in craft workshops and online communities, if you look for it.

Making Together

Participation in crafts enjoyed a huge surge during the pandemic. Some suddenly had time to get back onto their long-dormant projects and others tried new crafts for the first time. It did not go unnoticed that as industry ground to a halt, craft re-emerged, offering itself as a tool for endurance and resilience.

Despite the isolation of lockdown, many makers continued to engage with their craft community. Whether by exchanging Artist Trading Cards by post, or responding to daily themed prompts via social media, great importance was placed on staying connected and creative. Some marked the passing of time with 'inchies'; a low-pressure way to maintain regular practice on a tiny scale each day. An inch felt achievable, and though small, these daily efforts quickly accumulated, revealing unexpected progress over time. These small acts of making gave shape to unstructured days, and the collective effort evoked a sense of unity and hopefulness.

When social distancing steered us towards online learning, sharing stories became one of the main features of a class. As we worked and listened, the colours and the tactile feel of the materials offered a sensory connection – the stories became bonded to the making process, the details woven in with every thread. Now, despite returning to our usual routines post-pandemic, many of us have continued to make time for craft, both together and alone. It is pleasant to be around people with whom we share a common interest. Whether online or in person, there is always laughter and also times of quiet, when everyone is deep in the flow of their work.

When we attend a craft workshop, the new skills we learn are not the only thing we can expect to take away with us. Together we are a melting pot of ideas. If we are open, we can tap into a collective bank of knowledge, and between us, several diverse lifetimes of experience. We might learn of a new yarn shop to visit or a better way to tie a knot. Conversations might lead to book recommendations or a new recipe. Craft may be our starting point but conversations are fluid and rarely limited to the task at hand. We might just find that we have more in common than our love of making.

Chapter 3

The Value of Time Spent Making

Sometimes I am asked the questions: 'Why do this?' or 'What are they for?' I am asked this especially about my woven rocks – and I understand. What is the point if you can't use the fabric once it's been woven? Interestingly, we don't tend to ask this of paintings or sculptures, or of poetry, literature or music. Imagine having to find a functional use for a painting, to justify its creation.

When I asked other makers to share their thoughts on this, many reported feeling an obligation to use their skills only for making useful things. I sense that for many of us there is an ingrained idea that time spent making, especially if it's non-functional or for pleasure, is less well spent – self-indulgent, even. But why do we feel this way?

We live in a culture that celebrates productivity, speed and profit. We can't help but internalise the idea that the time we spend has to be 'worth it' in some physically or financially measurable way. But aren't we forgetting a) how valuable art and craft have been in the history of humankind and b) how important rest, expression and enjoyment are in our lives?

The importance we place on function goes back to past necessity – once upon a time we had to make useful things in order to survive. Our choice to continue making things today is one of privilege, but it also speaks to an innate human instinct to make things with our hands.

In contrast, some responders felt that reducing their creative abilities to making useful things devalued both them and the items. Some felt put off making functional items because of the risk that their value would be called into question when compared with cheaper commercial items. Others were afraid of using their handmade items in case they ruined them, preferring to display them as art.

It has taken a long time for textile art to be accepted as a proper form of art. It is thanks to pioneering artists such as Sheila Hicks, Tracey Emin, Anni Albers, Lenore Tawney, Magdalena Abakanowicz, Rosie Lee Tompkins, Gunta Stölzl, Hannah Ryggen, Theo Moorman and others who have put textile art and activism firmly on the map in more recent decades.

While weaving has historically been practised by both men and women, textile making is often still thought of predominantly as 'women's work', and I wonder whether this mindset creates a subconscious barrier about what can rightfully be considered art or craft.

Though first developed for its functionality, weaving has long been practised as a form of expression. Besides its many practical applications, it has been used to depict historic events, to make political statements, to raise awareness about social issues, to deal with grief and to express identity and the human experience.

Humans have always added decoration to a point beyond usefulness. It is in our nature to adorn ourselves and our surroundings with beauty. 'Ornament' is important to humans because it enriches life beyond functionality. The line between decorative and useful is sometimes blurred. A useful handmade item can light us up in the same way that a piece of art can. The process of stitching a quilt can be similar to stitching an artwork that will be framed for the wall. Weaving is a craft that can produce both items of use and items of art from the same warp. There is a spectrum.

One thing I am sure of is that weaving (and making in general) has more to offer than practical uses; its validity stretches far beyond keeping us warm and dry. When I first began to consider why it is that I like to weave, I imagined that my motivation was plain and simple – doing so brings me joy and peace – but as I looked closer I discovered that I could think of hundreds of reasons.

That's lovely, but what can it be used for?

The question 'But what can these be used for?' gives rise to another thought. Is it necessary for us to justify our choice to spend time on creative projects? If it isn't (spoiler, it isn't), why does it often feel like it is?

Sometimes, when I sit down to work on one of my weavings, I feel a pang of 'I should be doing something useful'. I'd describe it as enjoyment that is slightly tinged with anxiety. And I'm not the only one. I asked my community whether they felt craft was valued in today's society and I was pleasantly surprised at how many people said yes. However, when I asked whether they ever felt guilty about time spent crafting, many also said... yes. (I must also note here that some of the responders said they did not feel guilty – even reinforcing their 'no' by writing it in capital letters and adding a defiant exclamation mark – an absolute delight to hear.)

Those who elaborated on why they felt validated to spend time crafting said that:

- the people around them were supportive and encouraging of this
- their practice is a form of self-care
- they crafted with others, and together, they felt validated to spend their time this way.

Many participants felt that crafting is integral to their way of life. Some expressed awe at being able to do these things at all and said how wasteful it would be not to embrace that. But let's look a little deeper at the responses:

- Some responders expressed that they can justify the time spent crafting if the item they are making is useful.
- Others said that they feel less anxiety if they know they can exchange their end result for money.
- Of those who did express feelings of 'I should be doing something else', some felt more guilty about making during daylight hours, often saving their craft projects for evenings. (Even retirees found it hard to shake this feeling.)
- One responder described crafting as a 'reward', and they felt they must 'pay' for craft time by doing some other chore.
- More than one expressed guilt about wasting materials.
- Some felt that because craft is often seen as a 'woman's pursuit', the work is less valued, even by other women.

For many, making is a form of self-care, and self-care is of value. We often prioritise productivity over rest, but we cannot have one without the other. I can't help but wonder if the way we value time spent on craft mirrors broader cultural attitudes towards rest. In a society that prioritises productivity, rest often only feels acceptable when we frame it as 'recovery' in preparation for more work.

When learning to embrace slow craft today, it is hard to unlearn what we've been taught. I love the idea of 'rest' and 'making' as radical acts of resistance. One thing that those of us engaged in making can generally agree on is that for us, it is a deeply valuable, integral part of our lives. As Cal Newport puts it in his book *Digital Minimalism*, 'A life well lived requires activities that serve no other purpose than the satisfaction that the activity itself generates.'

Your choice to engage in making doesn't have to make sense to anyone else but you. Even if joy was the only benefit of crafting, that would be enough to justify spending time on it.

Stretching the Boundaries of Functionality

A 'functional' object is usually thought of as something that is useful in a practical sense. But if we reframe it another way, perhaps its meaning is subjective. In the context of making, functionality could mean many things, not least providing beauty, joy, learning and connection and as a vehicle for expression. If a piece is interesting, progressive, sparks conversation, contributes to culture, then I'd venture that it is serving a valuable purpose.

We don't always have to know why we are doing something. The reasons that certain things speak to us are sometimes unclear until later. To make the most of our curiosity and allow for open experimentation and discovery, it can be useful to remove the constraints of working towards a useable product.

Is It Art or Craft?

How do we identify whether our work is art, craft or design? Is it necessary for us to categorise our work at all? Sometimes our creative offerings don't fit neatly into a specific box and the need to find a label that fits can feel invalidating.

Though humans have been making things for millennia, some of the language we use to categorise 'types' of making is relatively new. Definitions of art, craft and design are fluid by nature, redefined constantly by artists and makers themselves, by the consumer and by the gradual evolution of culture and society. We may hold their definitions quite firmly in our minds, but upon closer inspection it is difficult to pinpoint exactly where the goalposts are. Sometimes the simple act of making can be a starting point that, if we allow ourselves to move freely, could lead on to art, craft, design, or something else entirely.

Blurred Lines

Like design, both art and craft can be appreciated for their formal elements; shape, form, colour, composition, balance and aesthetic. 'Craft' may be defined as skilful execution – but this can also be said of art making, and as such craft can embrace playfulness and expression, just like art. In the same way that art can tell us about our history, so too can handcrafted utilitarian objects and symbolic ornament. All are influenced by culture, and they contribute to it. It is a symbiotic relationship.

Here's another thought: something doesn't have to be labelled as 'art' to justify its non-functionality. When we identify that something doesn't have a utilitarian use, we might automatically justify its existence by saying 'it's decorative' or 'it's art.' It doesn't have to be either of those things. I didn't start making woven objects with the intention of making art. At the beginning, it was just that the process soothed my soul.

Sometimes, reducing exciting ideas to words and definitions can take something integral away from their magic. It is important that we do not bend or force our work out of shape in order for it to fit external ideas about what is valid.

If you are unsure whether your work falls within art, design or craft, all or none of the above, just know that whatever you're making, it is valid and has a place in this world.

Chapter 4

The Humanness of Making Things

'The maker in me is inseparable from the human, for it is what has distinguished us from other species'

- Nick Kary, *Material*

These days, we can easily buy the things we need. So why do so many of us still love to make our own, even though it takes longer and is often more expensive? As a maker myself I can tell you that we don't do it for the money; it is rarely enough.

I once heard a quote about rave culture that went something like this: 'You do not need to ask the question "Why do we rave?", the answer is obvious in the immediacy of the joy.' I think that says it all. Many of us feel compelled to make. We feel a pull towards it. We need to do it.

CLOVER

What Draws Us Towards the Need to Make?

When I have this conversation with others, the resounding response is that making is a basic human instinct, a fundamental, primordial urge. Rick Rubin, author of *The Creative Act*, compares this feeling to love and as 'a kinetic draw beyond our rational comprehension.' Let's delve a little deeper into what makes that so.

Instinct and Survival

Making and using tools was the very first thing we did that set us apart from other animals. Early humans used their hands to wield materials into useful objects of rock, clay, hide and fibre. We painted images on cave walls, of animals, of the stars, announcing our existence, depicting our way of life. We made useful objects to aid our survival and we used those same skills as a form of creative expression.

As an ancient craft, weaving is deeply connected to what it is to be a human. Like music, dancing, singing, painting and tool making, weaving developed independently in many parts of the world and likely predates written language. The industrialisation of craft and the rapid advances in technology we've seen over the past 200 years is actually an incredibly recent change when you consider the many, many thousands of years human beings have been making things with our hands. Human evolution takes millennia, so it's no wonder our instincts haven't caught up yet and many still feel this basic human instinct to wield materials.

Maybe deep in our evolutionary memory, the act of 'making' signals that we're doing what we need to survive. Back then, 'rest' would have been entirely dependent on us having created a safe environment for ourselves. When we feel safe, our nervous system can relax. On a subconscious level, the brain may still associate the act of making with self-sufficiency, resilience and preparedness.

▲ The Mid Essex Guild of Weavers, Spinners & Dyers

Reconnection

Making may not always have been as enjoyable an activity as it is today. For those who came before us, for whom it was a necessity, the labour would have been hard and the days long. Now, we have the privilege of choice but far fewer opportunities to embrace 'making' as part of our daily lives.

For many people today, making is a chance to reconnect with our humanness, despite the lack of necessity. In our fast-paced modern world, crafting could be described as a familiar friend, a security blanket, something that grounds us back to what we know when everything around us is changing and becoming more abstract.

The Power In Our Hands

Many of us feel a primordial urge to 'do something with our hands'. From the moment we are born, we explore the world through our senses. Taste, sight, smell, touch.

Hands are often described as 'man's first tools'. The tools we make are an extension of our hands, created by us, to further enhance our capabilities. When we make things, we connect our inner and outer worlds, building a bridge between the two. Our hands help us to translate an idea – something that exists only in our minds – into physical, tangible form. There is a satisfaction in watching the transformation from material to object happen through our hands. Through practice and repetition, our hands gain muscle memory and hold knowledge. We learn to respond instinctively to our materials, which allows us to work with precision.

A Connection to Past and Future

As Peter Korn expresses in *Why We Make Things and Why It Matters*, 'The best way to understand craft, I believe, is to think of it as a conversation flowing through time.' There may be times when we feel disconnected from generations even just one or two steps back or forward from our own, but craft is something that unites people of all ages. Though the makers of historic artefacts may have lived in a different century (or even millennia) to us, their objects offer relatability, for their human experiences still hold strong similarities to ours.

We often hear of art, craft, design and marketing referred to as a universal visual language, capable of expressing deep meaning, which can be felt across time and place. Every craft that is still enjoyed today is the result of the passing down of skills and knowledge. When we make things, we are learning from our ancestors and leaving clues for future generations.

Language and Communication

As Rick Rubin expresses in *The Creative Act*, 'Art has an ability to connect us beyond the limitations of language.' Creative expression is one of the rare times we get to experience another person's imagination in physical form. Looking at an object, a textile, or a piece of music someone has made offers us a glimpse into their inner world.

Sometimes spoken or written language isn't enough. Non-verbal communication allows us to connect and understand each other in different ways and in more depth, filling in the gaps. Creative expression is a language that connects us all. You don't have to be an artist or a maker to understand it, you just have to be human. Besides an object-making species, we are a storytelling one. Expressing a narrative through the things we make tells the world who we are. We put a little of ourselves into our work and we live on through our creations, even after we are gone.

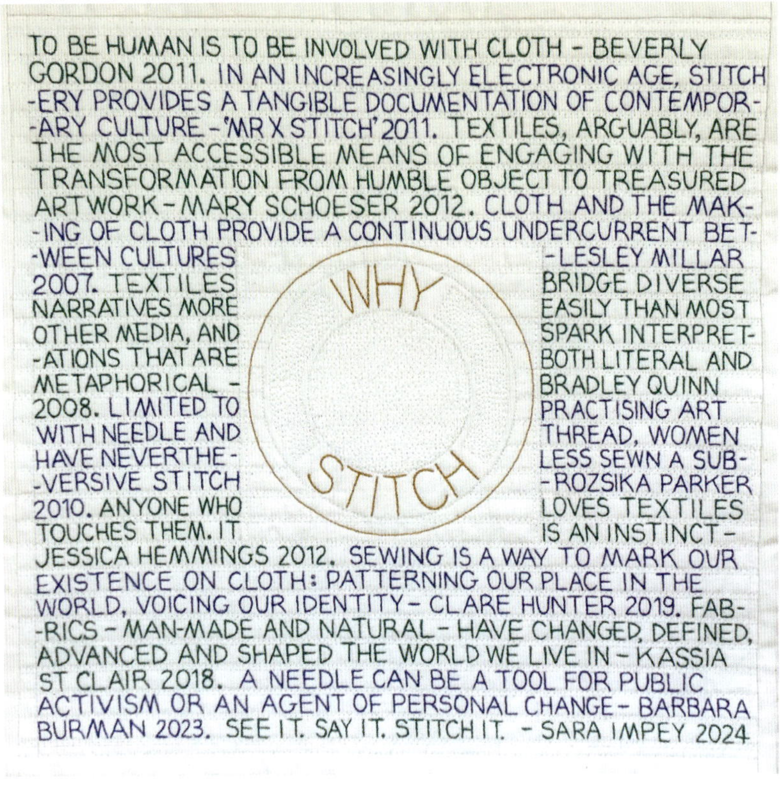

▲ *Why Stitch*, Sara Impey, 2024

Sara Impey has been making textile artworks based on the techniques of quiltmaking for most of her adult life, and for the last twenty years she has focused on stitching text, using free-motion machine embroidery. This calico wholecloth piece is 40 × 40cm (16 × 16in), crafted using free-motion machine embroidery and machine quilting. The drive to stitch seems to come from deep within her and she values the hours spent at the sewing machine, but it is sometimes difficult to explain this in a way that makes sense to non-stitchers. For some time, she has been collecting quotations from commentators from the wider textile world that articulate the significance of fabric and thread in all our lives, and some of them are stitched here. They are both validating and affirming.

Immortality and Purpose

The things we make may well outlive us. Objects that we make and pass down come to represent us – become us, even – before returning to the earth.

When we are making something for someone, thoughts of them pass through us with every stitch. We imagine giving it to them, we picture them wearing or using it. We are giving them part of ourselves to carry with them, and the time we have spent making it is time we have given to them.

Recently, my grandmother asked me what the perfect blanket to make for me would be. I asked for a colourful one. She was so excited and started straight away. A few weeks later we arranged the colourful squares on the floor, experimenting with different layouts, and she carefully considered the composition, the balance of colours. Then she sewed them all together, by hand, and finished it off with a beautiful red border edging. I will treasure this blanket for the rest of my life. When I wrap myself in it, I think of her and how miraculous it is that she still does this at ninety-nine. When I spend time with her I have the impression she is trying to curate for me a lasting memory of her. This blanket is a perfect representation: colourful, vibrant, full of life and a bit crackers.

On one of our 'crafternoons', my grandmother told me that she feels crochet has saved her. This may seem a dramatic statement to some, but it makes perfect sense to me. She finds the hand work calming, and she can still provide for her family and her community by giving her crochet blankets away to local care homes, hospices, or anyone who has recently had a baby. They are always received with such gratitude, and this makes her feel happy.

A-TEAM
Record Decs
Banner Making
TOYS
Fire action
BISLEY

Freedom

It can feel liberating to indulge in our own interests outside of our day-to-day responsibilities. In the modern workplace and our busy home lives, we don't often get to enjoy a feeling of completion between tasks. Often, we are already working towards the next goal before the current one has been achieved.

For many of us, handwork offers us a simpler, more grounding human experience. When we work on a self-directed craft project, we can enjoy the rare freedom and autonomy to make all of the decisions ourselves, from start to finish.

Passing on Skills

It occurs to me that we might be the last generation to have parents or grandparents who were serious craftspeople. That makes it all the more important to keep making and passing on those skills where we can.

We become better makers by teaching our craft. Having to articulate the how and the why of our work on a regular basis can help us to understand our own intention and motivations. The scope of our craft is greatly broadened by our students. When I teach, I feel very much a participant as the learning is mutually beneficial.

As a young professional the idea of sharing can feel vulnerable. However, for us to have made it this far into our creative journeys, multiple people will have generously shared their skills with us.

◀ Teaching with Berni Yates – a special teacher and friend who inspired and supported me from the beginning.

When we keep a tight hold on our ideas and skills, our creative impact stops with us. Passing on what we know doesn't lessen our value, it amplifies it. The continuation of craft depends on what we're willing to give, not what we keep to ourselves.

Valuable Life Skills

The benefits of making can last a lifetime. The creative skills we develop as children stay with us and continue to support us as we navigate adulthood. Yet, we rarely attribute these valuable life skills to our early experiences with craft. The link may not be obvious, but it is there.

When we are children, using our hands to explore materials and their limits teaches us problem-solving skills and resourcefulness. In low-pressure creative environments, we learn how to fail and rebuild. As we shape the materials around us, they too shape us. Our new-found knowledge about how materials behave and respond to our hands builds intuition, which can help us with decision making and planning.

Creative play helps us to form the neural pathways we need to build our imaginations. If this is nurtured in childhood, we are more likely to become creative or even abstract thinkers as adults. As we make our way through life, picking up new creative skills along the way, we accumulate a bank of knowledge that we can draw from again and again. Into adulthood, making can be a welcome respite from the strain of day-to-day responsibilities. Continued practice in older age helps us to maintain those skills, keeping our brains active and engaged, and keeping us social.

'Thinking Through Making'

While researching for this book, I noticed that the idea of 'thinking through making' and 'thinking with our hands' is frequently referenced by multiple artists and craftspeople. For me, the time I spent weaving greatly informed my writing; the rhythms of the process seemed to unlock barriers in my brain, allowing me to better articulate concepts that previously felt scattered and fragmented. The act of weaving helped me to find the connections and piece them together in a cohesive way. Somehow, the making process seems to garner perspective – as our hands work the materials, our brains pave a way through to a kind of clarity.

The Joy of Total Immersion

Have you ever felt totally in the zone while crafting? When I am immersed in my work, time seems to pass differently. I am in a bubble, outside of which nothing else exists. Noises go unnoticed; thirst, hunger, worries – none of the usual distractions seem to penetrate. When I am in this state, I feel an energy in my belly – colours appear more vivid, textures more delightful. The only sound is my needle as it pulls through the fabric, the plucking of warp threads as I count in threes.

According to studies, this state is most achievable when working on something repetitive or familiar that demands just enough focus to distract us from our cares but offers enough of a challenge to keep us engaged. When we are in a creative flow, we get into a rhythm, a trancelike state. We become lost in the work.

The link between crafting and well-being has been known for many hundreds, if not thousands of years, despite its lack of recognition in the medical field. Craft is often recommended by occupational therapists as a treatment for stress, depression, anxiety, grief and physical ailments. Immersing ourselves in creative activity allows us to set aside our troubles temporarily, creating space for joy and a sense of accomplishment to emerge.

While sports and exercise are widely recognised for their positive impact on mental health and overall wellness, crafting offers an accessible alternative – particularly when more physically demanding activities are not feasible. Many crafts can be enjoyed while resting, making them an ideal aid to recovery and self-care.

Textiles in Activism

Sometimes the world can feel like a scary place. Art can be a welcome reprieve – but it can also be a tool to help us to reimagine a better future. Art can challenge social norms. In fact, art that was 'banned' or has previously caused outrage and controversy often turns out to be a powerful catalyst for change.

Textiles have long been used in protest. Due to the association between cloth and women's work, including a textile element in protest can make the cause feel more approachable and safer, offering a disarmingly powerful way to reach people. Large-scale textiles can be incredibly impactful. Flags, banners, signs, tents, clothing – textiles hold

physical space and capture attention. Finding creative ways to communicate complex ideas makes them more accessible and memorable.

Creating textiles for use in peaceful protest can also be an opportunity for people to craft together, sharing knowledge, experiences and stories as they work. The social bonds created through joint effort imbue protest pieces with power and meaning, transforming them into symbols of solidarity – all of which can help to conjure the hope, motivation and bravery needed to speak out and make a stand.

The *Coat of Hopes* is an ever-evolving community-created patchwork coat made on a walk of nearly 2000 miles so far. On 30 August 2021, the then blank coat set out on a nine-week walk from the south coast of England to COP26 in Glasgow. The 'pilgrims' were sheltered and fed by community centres and churches along the way. Local people were invited to make patches expressing their hopes, prayers, griefs and remembrances in the face of climate breakdown. These were stitched onto the coat at stops along the way. At the gates of COP26, delegates were invited to wear the coat as an act of solidarity before stepping inside to become a part of decision making for our future, to impress upon them their responsibility and accountability to life on earth. However, in the light of their inability to make adequate change a reality, the coat continues to travel the country, inviting all to wear it, and to grow as more patches are added. The coat itself is a joint effort by hundreds of makers and walkers.

Awe and Wonder

Arts and crafts were here before us and will outlive us. Being creative isn't just something we do on an individual level, it's something we do collectively as a species – it's part of the human experience. In the end it's not about 'the work' or how good it is, it's about how you feel. It's not about 'progressing design', it's about reconnecting with yourself as a human being.

The why of it, for me, comes back to the meaning that it brings to our lives. The peace, the joy, that sense of purpose, the freedom, the community, the connection, the humanness. We don't need to make things (I say this, rolling my eyes), but we do, sort of, need to (and I say this with both hands on my heart). There is a maker in us all.

▶ *Coat of Hopes*, outside St Georges Tron, Glasgow, 2021

coat of hopes
HOPE
HAVE HOPE
TREES

Chapter 5

Approaching a New Craft

Before you begin your first exploration into off-loom weaving, I'd like to invite you to approach it with curiosity and playfulness. There is something inevitable that happens when learning this craft. At some point, you will realise you have made a small mistake a few rows back. All that hard work! I know. I am well acquainted with this frustration and cannot stress enough how normal this is, and how necessary. There is value in mistakes if you allow them to be an opportunity for learning.

Often, the mistake is something tiny that only you as a maker could ever spot. Here, we are divided into two camps: those who must go back and correct the error and those who embrace it. For those of us in the first camp, leaving the error in is out of the question – knowing it is there bugs us, visible or not. Others seem to take it in their stride, enjoying the uniqueness it brings to the piece.

Either way, the benefit was in making the mistake in the first place. Both options for how to move forward offer something positive. If you want to better understand the structure or pattern you are learning, it can be useful to go back and see if you can figure out how to correct it. Equally, if you can allow a 'mistake' to exist in your work, you are doing what many cannot. Embracing errors is brave and freeing, and makes space for spontaneity and discovery. In doing so you widen your scope of possibilities and do good work in dispelling the importance of perfection.

Remember, only you know what your intentions were with the piece. When we see an object or a piece of art for the first time, we have no knowledge of what the artist's original intentions were; whether they stuck to their plan or allowed their idea to evolve as they went along. If we do spot an imperfection, we often see beauty in it – it indicates to us that somebody made this with their hands and poured hours of their time into it.

Sometimes new things can be discovered by going wrong. If there is a fault or a mistake in the structure, or if the count of threads in a warp stripe was one less or one more than it should have been, you might just discover a new pattern! This is the magic of weaving. With practice, you might even find a better technique than the one you have been taught; your own method for hiding the knots or loose threads, or a better way to compact the wefts after each row. You'll be surprised how much you will teach yourself, filling in the gaps of learning.

Working with children has been one of the most inspiring and beneficial aspects of my teaching experience. They are not constrained by correctness – they absorb a little of the process and combine it with playfulness and inventiveness. The outcomes are pure joy. When I spend time with children, I am reminded to be playful myself. Embracing wonkiness and mistakes is enlightening and freeing.

▶ A weaving by one of the students from A-Team Arts Education, an East London based youth arts organisation.

Progress Blindness and Building Confidence

Sometimes, when we have spent a long time working on something, staring at it hour after hour makes it difficult to judge progress. We begin to ask ourselves: 'Is it good or is it rubbish? I can't tell anymore!' Putting it away and coming back to it another time can help us to view it with fresh eyes, to see its quality more clearly. Often, we find we have accomplished more than we thought.

For many people, fear of failure stops us from trying things at all. We want to skip the scary part and be good at it already. When we view art in a gallery we don't get to see all the failed attempts that the artist has pushed through before the masterpiece is conceived. We don't witness the perseverance, the lifetime of learning. We must allow ourselves to see value in our first attempts; to remove pressure and to embrace mistakes as part of our journey. There is nothing more inspiring than seeing a clear progression in our work, and that cannot happen if it is perfect from the beginning.

Often, in our eagerness to master a craft, we overlook the magic of the process itself, the unfolding journey that can sustain and inspire us for a lifetime.

Bending the Rules

Learning and practising is repetitive work, but once we've nailed it we can start to bend the rules and get creative. What if I reverse the order of the wefts? What if I do the opposite of what it says in the instruction? A surprise pattern, an unusual texture, a new idea. Sometimes the fun begins when we let go of how things are 'supposed to be done'; to find a way back to play.

The idea in your head is always the perfect version of the piece. If it feels like the real thing is falling short, it can be tempting to give up. Instead, try to embrace whatever surprise is emerging from each step. With weaving, it is particularly difficult to visualise how combinations of colour, material and structure will look together, and often the end result is quite different from the imagined one.

When we are making, our brains are engaged with our hands and eyes, receiving a steady flow of visual and textural feedback. This constant input and output of information naturally causes our ideas to evolve from moment to moment. Trying to control the outcome too much can put a ceiling on your creativity, so 'go with it' as much as you can.

Chapter 6

Sourcing Yarn

You don't have to spend the earth to try this craft – you might already have everything you need at home. My first off-loom weaving was made with a piece of cardboard and some leftover cottons that I found in the bottom of a drawer (see page 220).

If you're like me, and you have a 'laterbase' of small amounts of yarn or scraps that 'might come in handy one day', this craft is for you. If not, this is your sign to start keeping leftovers for potential use later – even if it's just to stuff a cushion with at some point. Besides saving money, it feels nice to give a second life to previously redundant materials instead of sending them to landfill. Leftover threads are also great for practice before moving on to a more intentional design. As is often the way when you are part of a textile community, if you let it be known that you like to use second-hand yarn, some may well find its way to you. I've also listed some places at the back of the book that might be helpful (see pages 222–23).

MACKIE'S
PITCAITHLY
SHORTBREAD

Second-hand Yarns

Using second-hand yarn adds depth to a piece. As we make use of remnants, we might think about the friends or family members who have gifted their precious materials to us. Even if we don't know the previous owners, we feel a connection to them through an obvious shared love of craft. We might wonder about the vision someone might have had for them, and why they were eventually discarded, and what our intentions are with them.

◀ Recently, someone that I once bought a loom from got in touch to see if I wanted her 'warp ends' that she had saved from recent weaving projects. Small amounts like these are perfect for off-loom weaving.

Caring for Second-hand Yarns

It can be useful to keep second-hand yarn in a sealed bag for a few days or even put it in the freezer to eliminate any larvae or moths from getting to the rest of your precious supply. Though it can be tempting to unwrap and display your beautiful threads, it can be safer to keep them in something airtight until you are ready to use them and you are certain there are no critters hiding.

When receiving warp ends or leftover scraps, twist them or make yarn balls out of them to keep them from tangling. I often rewrap opened embroidery floss skeins onto pieces of cardboard if they have lost their paper holders.

Sourcing Industry-waste Yarn

Besides making use of second-hand materials from other makers, another option is to seek out yarn that has been discarded by industry. Having worked in the textile industry in various capacities I've become aware of the sheer quantity of new yarn that's produced every year, and also how much is wasted during the manufacturing process.

We all know that tonnes of clothing end up in landfill each year, but did you know that perfectly good cones of yarn end up there too, before they've even had a chance to become a garment? There are many reasons yarn gets chucked away by textile mills and manufacturers: old stock that didn't get used, low-demand colours that have sat on the shelves too long, discontinued lines, cancelled orders, last season's colours. Manufacturers will often over-order yarn to meet fluctuating demand, to account for imperfections or to cover colour-matching losses.

Some machines, such as industrial warp winders, can only be loaded with full cones of yarn. This eliminates the need for intermittent stopping to replace the cones that have run out. The 'half cones' or 'end cones' that are left over at the end often become redundant, and these small amounts are wasted.

Many mills donate their leftovers to schools and universities, but there is often too much of it to give away. Luckily, here in the UK, there are a few places that resell industry-waste yarn to the craft community and to the general public. After all, a 'half cone' may not be much to a manufacturer, but to a crafty maker it can be enough to see us through many projects.

Fairfield Yarns, Lancashire

Fairfield Yarns is a family business run by David Fox, who has worked in the textile industry for thirty years. Having worked as a salesman for a yarn merchant earlier on, David noticed a demand from small businesses for industry-waste yarn. He started buying discarded and redundant stock from mills and reselling it to designers, students, teachers, textile studios and craftspeople, as well as resupplying it back into the textile industry. This has helped to mitigate waste created by industry.

The beauty of David's shop is not only the endless variety of fibres, colours, thicknesses, twists and textures but also David's encyclopaedic knowledge of yarn and of the industry. He is kind and gentle in his explanations of 'textile jargon', i.e. thread counts, and the meaning of 'nm', 'ply' and other yarn-measuring metrics.

When I first set foot in the door, I felt I had entered a magical place. Imagine an old second-hand bookshop, shelves jampacked from floor to ceiling, extra piles of books in every corner... except instead of books, it's cones of yarn of all kinds.

When you buy waste yarn, you may not find exactly the same yarn again. Once it's gone, it's gone. By now I know which yarns David usually has continuous stock of, but there is always something new, a surprise yarn that he has come into the possession of, that he has never had before and is unlikely to find again.

Other Sources

Besides Fairfield Yarns, here in the UK we also have:

- **Colourmart**, Shrewsbury – specialises in more luxurious industry-waste threads like cashmere, merino and angora.
- **Uppingham Yarns**, between Peterborough and Leicester – sells a mix of ex-industry yarns and new and novelty yarns from various suppliers.

For US crafters:

- **Old Mill Yarn**, Michigan – a great source for mill end yarn.
- **Fabcycle** – Collects textile waste from local mills, including scraps, dead stock and offcuts, and makes it available for reuse.

See if there are any mills or textile factories near you. Try getting in touch with them directly to ask if they have any yarn that is destined for the bin. They may agree to sell it to you, as this is mutually beneficial, providing them with a positive solution for their waste.

If you are searching online, try using keywords like 'industry-waste yarn', 'ex-industry yarn', 'dead stock yarn', 'redundant stock yarn' and 'surplus yarn'. eBay usually has some good options, too.

Chapter 7

Sourcing Bases

There are not many rules when it comes to choosing a base for off-loom weaving. The main two pointers are that the object must:

- Have four straight-*ish* edges
- Be strong enough to support threads being wrapped both vertically and horizontally without bowing, bending or snapping.

EMARY
BOOTS
AUDIO
C60

Wood

I often use offcuts donated from local wood workers and furniture makers in my work (the ones stacked here were donated by Rewthink). It's worth looking to see if you have one nearby, as their discarded bits and pieces are often already great sizes and shapes for weaving around – and you might be able to sample a few different wood types. Plus, you are also offering other makers a solution for some of their waste. It's a win-win!

Wood workers are also very knowledgeable on wood care, so make sure you ask about that too. A little oil can go a long way in protecting the wood long term, helping it to support your threads for longer.

Found Objects

Your base certainly doesn't have to be a perfectly oiled piece of wood. Materials that participants of my workshops and I have used as bases for weaving over the years include:

- Rocks
- Driftwood
- Wall or roof tiles
- Slate
- Brick
- Old coasters or placemats
- Old books or notebook covers
- Cassette tape, CD or LP covers
- Juice cartons
- Perspex or glass
- Thick cardboard or packaging materials.

Skip Diving

I often find myself at our local recycling centre, perusing the building rubble. You never know what treasures you might find.

Our recycling centre has a 'dump shop' for discarded items that are a little too good to go in the main refuse containers. I found a box of beautiful old Japanese tiles there – too few to be used for their original purpose but perfect for my 'white project' (see page 123).

Teachers, it's worth checking to see if there are any 'Scrap Projects' or 'Scrapstores' nearby. These are often charity-run organisations that collect waste from businesses and redistribute it as arts and crafts supplies. Membership is available to schools, universities, community centres and other groups to help provide young people with a diverse variety of materials to use as they develop their creative skills.

Once you've had a go at this craft, you will begin to see potential in everything. Every walk in nature, every trip to a charity shop, every skip in someone's driveway...!

Tip If you go skip diving, be careful of sharp broken edges. Wear gloves and be sure that you know what you are fishing out – I once unknowingly wove around a piece of asbestos!

▶ You never know what you might find on the side of the road.

Chapter 8

Twill

Twill is one of the oldest woven structures in the world. Evidence of early use dates back thousands of years – though in place of long-perished physical examples, imprints of the fabric left behind in clay have been discovered in multiple places across the globe. It won't always have been called twill – it is said that this name comes from the old English word *twili*, which in turn came from the Latin word *bilix* meaning 'two threaded'.

The diagonal interlacing of threads makes for a dense, strong, durable cloth with a beautiful drape that is a little more resistant to creasing – the perfect partner to this particular type of off-loom weaving. This book might as well have been called *A Love Affair with Twill* given how central it has become in my work.

Within the following projects you will learn how to weave a twill, but before we dive in with needle and thread, let's try first with paper.

Project 1

Paper Weaving 2/2 Twill

Structure

The 2/2 twill is named as such because the wefts are woven under 2, then over 2, then under 2, then over 2.

- Each row is slightly staggered from the last, which creates the diagonal pattern. This also means that each row begins and ends differently.
- The pattern repeats every **4** rows.
- The vertical strips are the warp, and the horizontal strips are the wefts.
- This simulation can be read from right to left or from left to right, depending on your handedness.

You Will Need

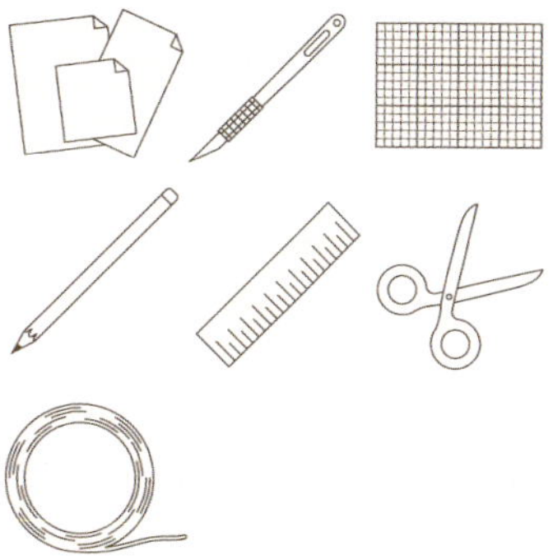

- A variety of colourful paper or card – mine is A4 cut in half (4 x 5¾in)
- Craft knife
- Cutting mat
- Pencil
- Ruler
- Scissors
- Tape

Steps

1 Use a craft knife, ruler and cutting mat to cut a piece of card or paper to any size you like to use as your warp. Using a pencil and ruler, draw a line about 1.5cm (⅝in) down from the top edge.

2 Use the ruler and craft knife to cut strips downwards from the line so that all of the warp strips remain connected at the top. It helps if the total number of warp strips is divisible by four; I have sixteen warp strips in total. Make sure that the strips are well separated.

3 Cut some strips to use for your wefts. These need to be a little longer than the width of your warp so that they stretch all the way across, with 1cm (⅜in) or so to spare each side. These need to be cut completely separate from one another, as singular strips. Now your warp and weft strips are ready to go.

4 Lay a strip of tape along the top edge to secure the warp to the table, so it doesn't move around while you are weaving. Now it's time to start weaving.

Weft 1

5 If you're right-handed, come in from the right and feed the first weft strip **under 2**, then over 2, under 2, over 2. Keep going all the way across.

If you're left-handed, feed the weft strip in from the left, beginning with **over 2**.

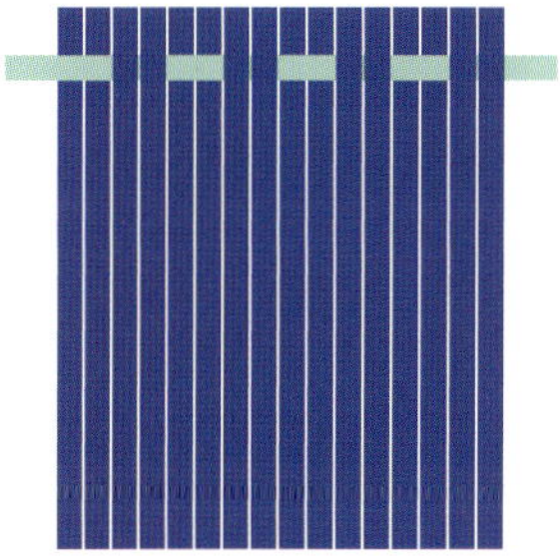

6 Push this weft right up to the top.

Weft 2

7 If you're right-handed, begin with **over 1 at the edge**, then back to under 2, over 2, under 2, over 2, all the way across, ending with over 1.

If you're left-handed, feed the weft strip in from the left, beginning the row with over 1, then under 2, over 2 and so on.

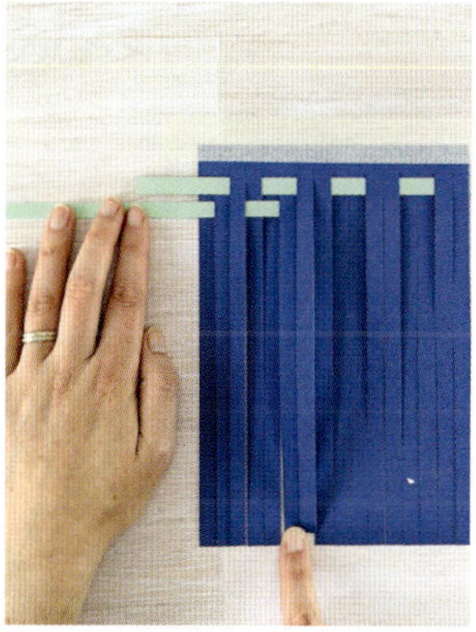

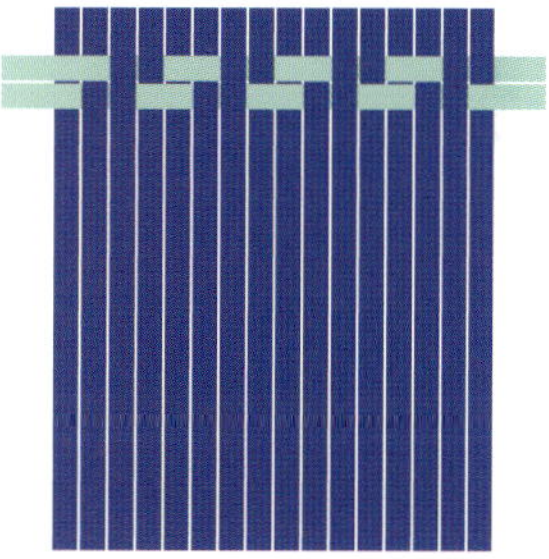

8 Push this weft right up to join the previous one.

Weft 3

9 Right-handers begin with **over 2 at the edge**, then under 2, over 2, under 2, over 2, all the way across.

Left-handers come in from the left, beginning with **under 2**.

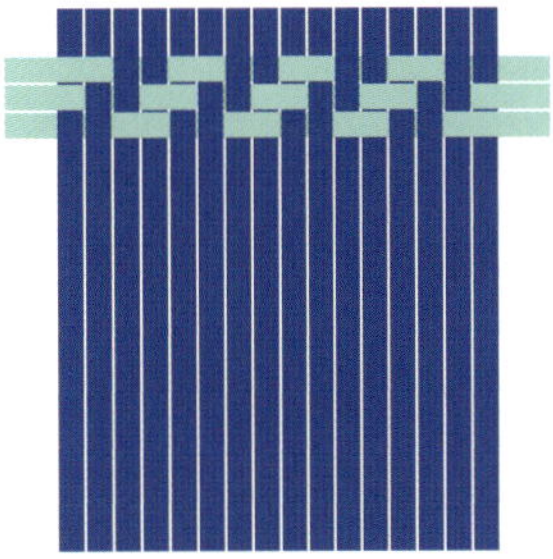

10 Push this weft right up to join the others at the top.

Weft 4

11 Right-handers begin this row with **under 1 at the edge**, then it's back to over 2, under 2, over 2, under 2 all the way across, ending the row with under 1.

Left-handers come in from the left, beginning with **under 1**.

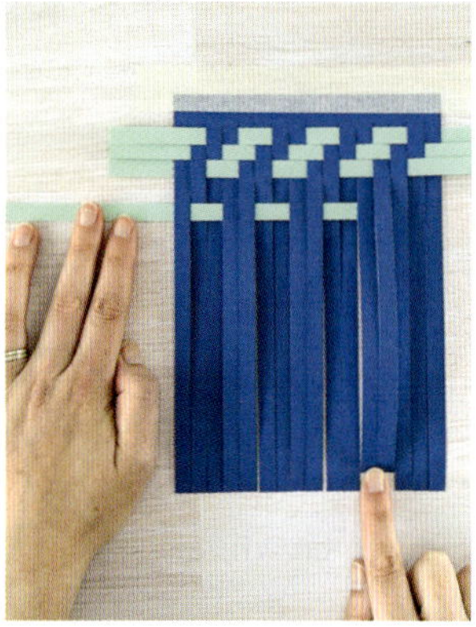

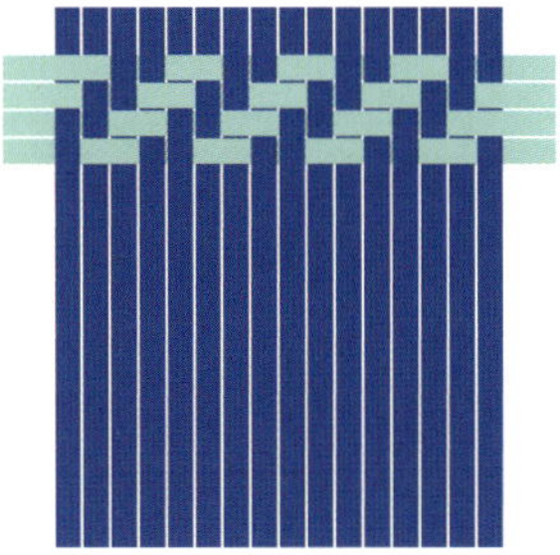

12 Push this weft right up to join the others at the top. Now you have completed one whole sequence of the pattern.

13 Start from **weft 1** and repeat the same sequence again...

14 ...and again. As you continue to repeat those same four wefts, you will see that the diagonal pattern continues seamlessly. Keep going until you reach the bottom, leaving a little space (about the same amount as the top) to create a nice even border around your weaving.

Extras To Try

If you add different colours into the warp and the weft, you can achieve all sorts of patterns. Look at the examples here – and remember, the structure is exactly the same, just the placement of colours is different.

▲ If you weave in stripes of '4 dark, 4 light' in both the warp and the weft, a dogtooth pattern will appear.

▲ This time, every strip of paper is a different colour.

▲ Here, the warp strips and weft strips are ordered '1 light, 1 dark, 1 light, 1 dark'.

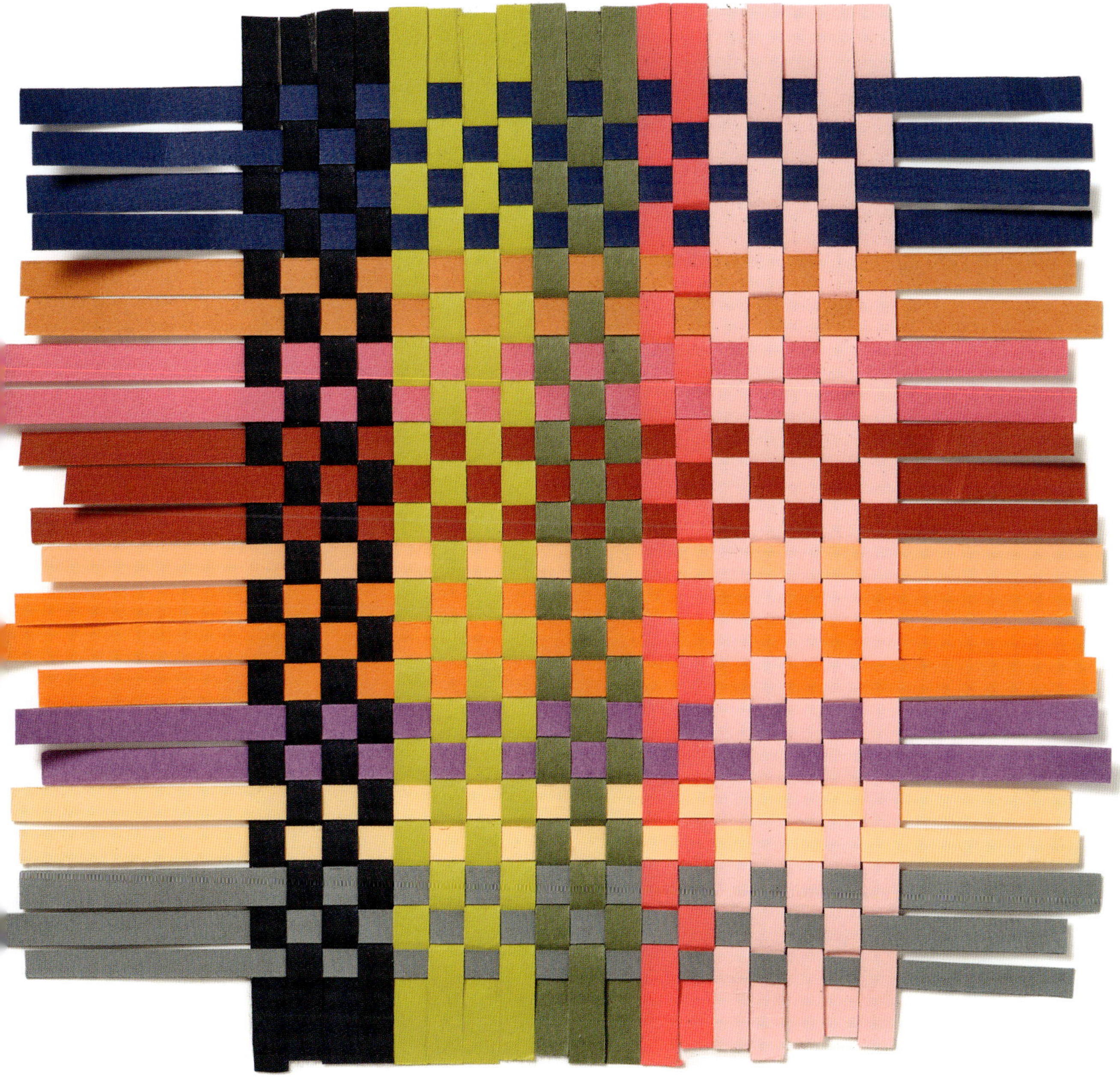

▲ You don't have to use twill to create an impactful artwork – this example is woven in a 'plain weave' structure, which is simply 'over 1, under 1' all the way through!

Project 2

3/3 Twill

It's time to weave with needle and thread. This time, we'll try the 3/3 twill. It's the same format as the 2/2 twill, except it's under **3**, and over **3**.

Structure

The 3/3 twill is named as such because the wefts are woven under 3, then over 3, then under 3, then over 3.

- Each row is slightly staggered from the last, which creates the diagonal pattern.
- As before, each row begins and ends differently.
- This pattern repeats every 6 threads.
- The simulation can be read from right to left or from left to right, depending on your handedness.

You Will Need

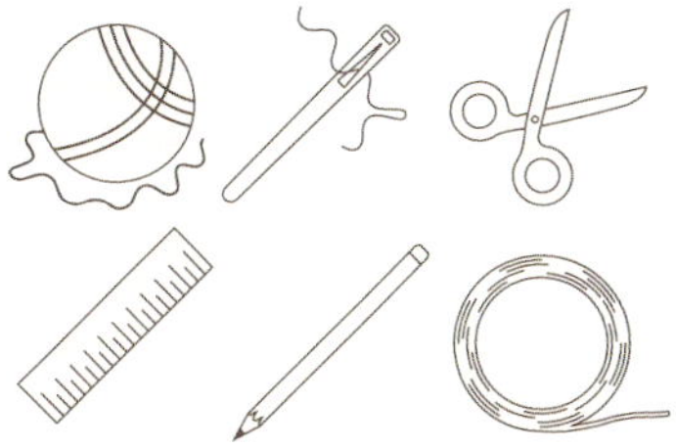

- Base (square or rectangle) – mine is A6 (approximately postcard sized) and 5mm (¼in) in thickness
- Yarn in **two contrasting colours** – I have used thick rug wool, but you can use whatever you like
- Needle
- Scissors
- Ruler
- Pencil
- Double-sided adhesive tape

Steps

Tip Before you begin, choose a comfy spot with good light. During, make sure to get up and stretch. Remember to stretch your eye muscles too – look away into the distance every now and then to give your eyes a rest.

Tip It is better to cut the tape rather than tear it, because it will be easier to lift the backing strips off from a sharp corner. Don't use your best fabric scissors, as the tape is sticky.

1 Make some marks on the **back** of your base to use as a guide for where to start wrapping the warp (vertical) threads and where to stop. I have marked 2cm (¾in) from each edge, along the top and bottom. You can make up your own measurements to best suit the size of your base.

2 As my base is rectangular, I've marked 2.5cm (1in) in from the edges on the long sides. (If the base was square, I would use the same measurements on all four sides.) These marks indicate where to start weaving in our weft (horizontal) threads and where to stop.

3 Lay some strips of double-sided tape longways between the two pencil lines. This is the back of your piece, so none of this will show on the front. If you would rather not use tape, skip this step. The wrapping process is the same with or without tape, it just adds a little extra security for the threads.

4 If you are right-handed, peel the first couple of backing strips off on the right-hand side.

If you are left-handed, peel the left two off.

5 It's time to wrap your 'warp' threads vertically around your boards. No need to cut a length of thread, just take the end of your chosen thread and lay it down **diagonally** onto the sticky tape on the back, angling it towards the top-right marker. If you're not using tape, just hold the end down with your thumb for the first few wraps.

If you are left-handed, attach the thread diagonally towards the top-left marker.

Tip If you don't have fingernails to pick the backing strips off, use the sharp end of a needle or the corner of a metal ruler. Don't peel them all off at once, as you don't want your thumb to stick to the board as you're winding.

6 Start wrapping your yarn around the board, laying each thread one after the other. Gradually the wrapped threads will cover and trap the diagonal 'end thread', securing it in place. Keep wrapping, maintaining a good even tension all the way across the warp. If you aren't using tape, it should now be safe to let go with your thumb. The wrapped threads will keep the end in place.

7 Peel off the backing strips as you go. Try not to allow the threads to overlap – wrapping them side by side will make the weaving process easier. There is no need to count the threads, just wrap until you reach the pencil line.

8 When you reach the marker, stop wrapping. Cut the thread but leave enough length to thread your needle, as you will be tucking this end behind the other warp threads on the back to secure it.

9 Keep your finger on the last wrapped thread to stop it from unwrapping, and use your other hand to position the needle under a few of the threads on the back. Thread the needle, still keeping your finger in place. This will help to keep everything tight and secure as you pull the thread through.

10 For as little extra security, go back a couple of threads and pass the needle under a few more. Pull it through again to create a small loop.

11 Make as many loops as you want until you feel the end is secure, then trim any excess thread away.

12 Cut a length of thread to use as your weft yarn – 1m (39in) is a good length to begin with. Too short a thread can run out too quickly, whereas too long a thread can become unmanageable when pulling it through. Thread the needle.

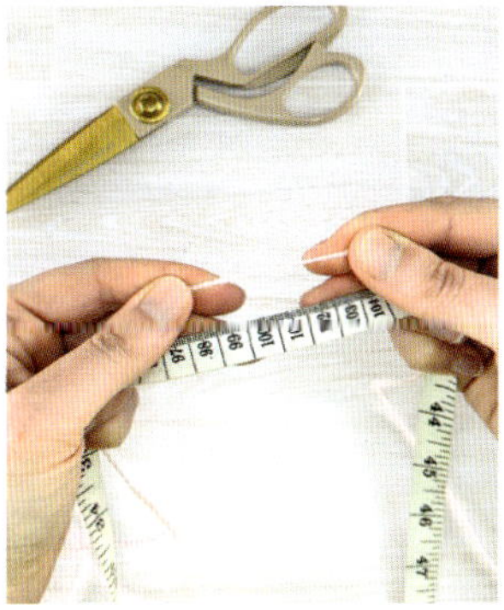

Tip If it's your first time weaving, using a thicker yarn will help you to clearly see what you're doing.
A flat 'bodkin' needle is great for weaving, but a regular sharp one is fine too.

13 Attach one end of the thread to the back of the board, using the looping technique from Step 10. Now turn your board over so that the front faces you.

Weft 1

14 **Right-handers**, coming in from the top right, begin the row with **under 3 at the very edge**, then over 3, under 3, over 3, under 3, all the way across.

Left-handers, coming in from the left, begin the row with over **3 at the edge**, then under 3, over 3, under 3, over 3, all the way across.

15 Don't feel you must go all the way across in one go; just go over and under as many as you can manage with your needle, then pull the thread all the way through before continuing. Make your way along the row, weaving over and under in stages. Take your time counting in threes – it's easy to accidentally go over 4 or under 2, for example. Pull the thread through carefully to avoid ending up with a knot.

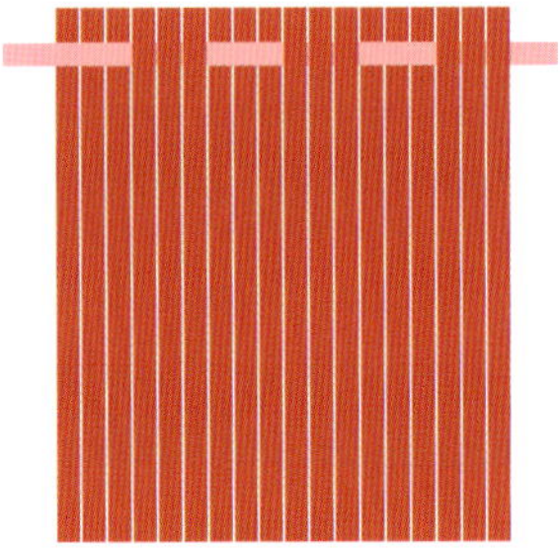

16 This is what your first weft should look like. Don't worry if you don't end on an 'over 3' like in the simulation – how your row ends will depend on how many warp threads you have wound around your board. My row ended with 'under 1', because that's all that was left. In fact, every row will begin and end differently because each row is slightly staggered from the last, which creates the diagonal pattern.

17 Now wrap the thread around the back, and bring the thread back around to the front, ready to start your next row.

Weft 2

18 **Right-handers**, come in from the right with over 1 at the edge, then it's back to under 3, over 3, under 3, over 3, all the way across.

Left-handers, come in from the left with over 2 at the edge, then back to under 3, over 3, under 3, over 3 and so on.

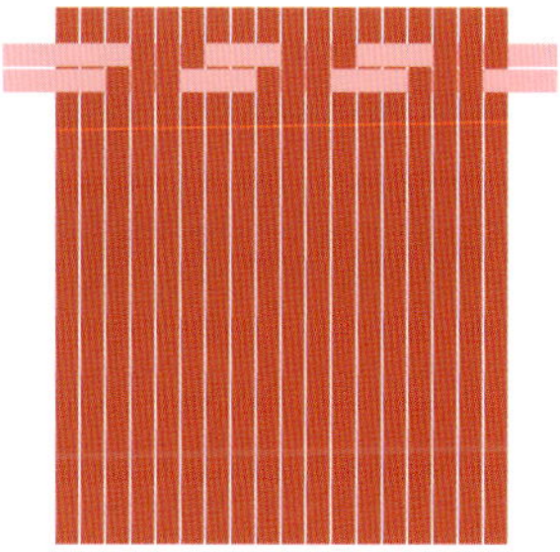

19 Weave the second row, bit by bit, and pull the thread all the way through. Use the needle to push the rows together, compacting them as much as you can and keeping them as straight as possible.

Weft 3

20 **Right-handers**, come in from the right with over 2 at the edge, then it's back to under 3, over 3, under 3, over 3, all the way across.

Left-handers, come in from the left with over 1 at the edge, then back to under 3, over 3, under 3, over 3 and so on.

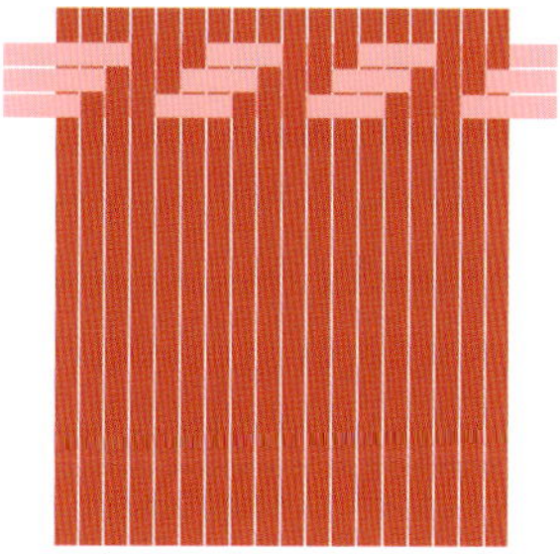

Weft 4

21 **Right-handers,** come in from the right with over 3 at the edge, then it's back to under 3, over 3, under 3, over 3, all the way across.

Left-handers, come in from the left with under 3 at the edge, then back to over 3, under 3, over 3, under 3 and so on.

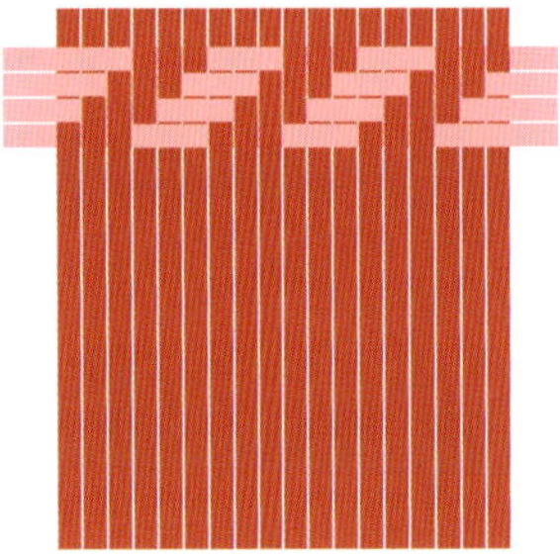

Weft 5

22 **Right-handers**, come in from the right with under 1 at the edge, then it's back to over 3, under 3, over 3, under 3, all the way across.

Left-handers, come in from the left with under 2 at the edge, then back to over 3, under 3, over 3, under 3 and so on.

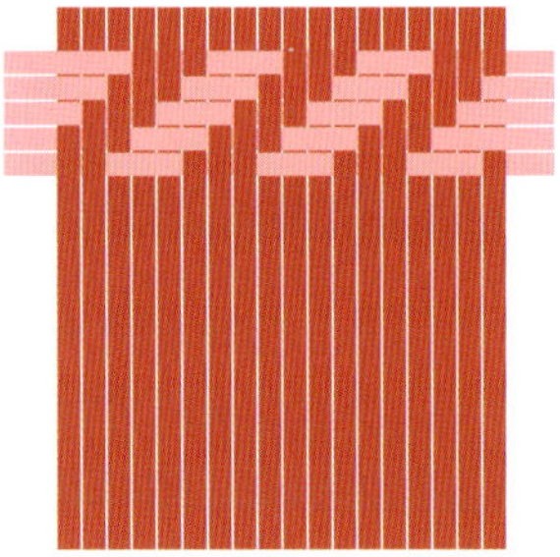

Weft 6

23 **Right-handers**, come in from the right with under 2 at the edge, then it's back to over 3, under 3, over 3, under 3, all the way across.

Left-handers, come in from the left with under 1 at the edge, then back to over 3, under 3, over 3, under 3 and so on.

That's one complete sequence of the 3/3 twill done.

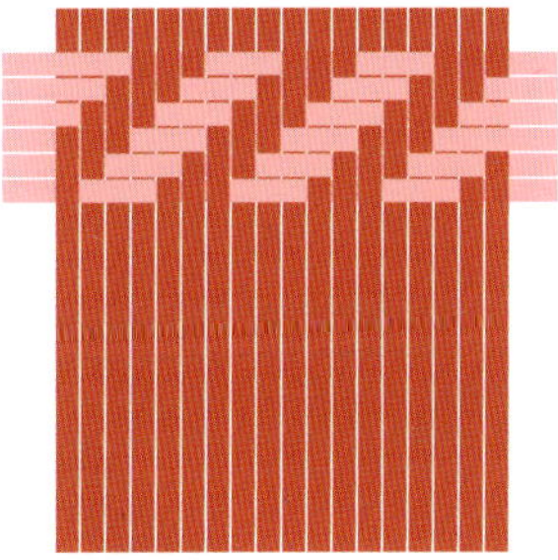

24 When you run out of thread, pass the end under some of the threads on the back. Use the looping technique to secure the end on the back of the board. Then cut a new length of thread and attach it in the same way as before. If you want to, you can use this opportunity to change to a new colour.

25 Now begin from weft 1 again.

26 Repeat all six rows again, and the pattern will continue seamlessly.

27 This is how your piece will look once you have completed three repeats of the pattern.

28 Keep going until you reach the pencil mark at the bottom. Here's your finished twill.

Tip At the end, you may find that your weaving has shifted off to one side a little. This is due to the repeated 'pulling through' of each weft thread, and is easily remedied by using your needle to shift the threads back over, bit by bit, until they are straight again.

29 Turn the piece over so that you're looking at the back. Pass the thread under a few of the wrapped threads on the back of the board, and loop it around a couple of times. Trim any remaining yarn away.

Weaving a Zigzag Pattern

1 If you want to create a zigzag, all you need to do is change the direction of your twill. The simulation below shows a direction change after one full repeat of the twill (after six wefts). Notice down the sides, the numbers are now 1, 2, 3, 4, 5, 6, then back down the scale with 5, 4, 3, 2, 1. Then back up the scale with 2, 3, 4, 5, 6 and so on. The simulation below (bottom) shows a direction change after two repeats of the twill (after twelve wefts).

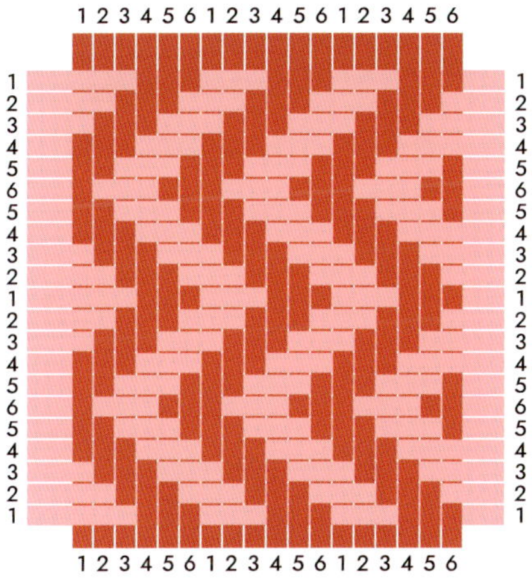

2 Here, I've completed two repeats of the twill. Having completed weft 6, go back to weft 5, then 4, 3, 2, 1, etc.

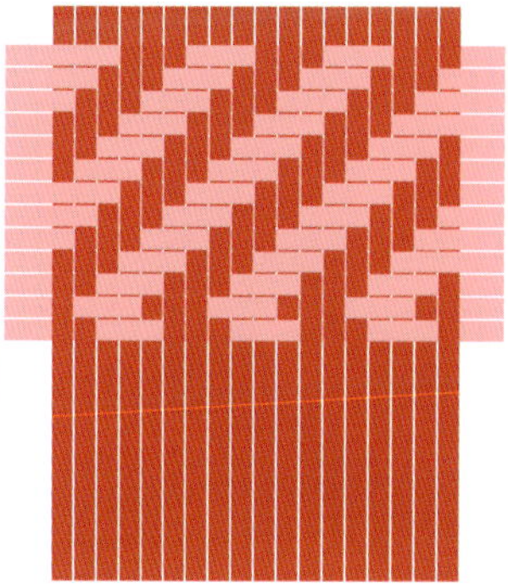

3 Like before, each row is moved one along from the last.

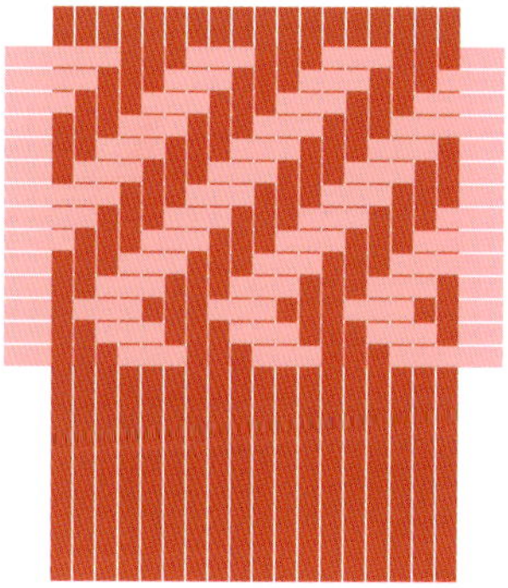

4 Can you see the disruption to the pattern?

5 You can change direction at any time – you don't have to stick to the simulation.

6 This is how your finished zigzag might look. When you've finished your weaving, the end of the last thread must be secured in place on the back, following Steps 29 above.

▲ Try combining a stripe and a zigzag.

Extras To Try

▼ Now you can change direction, try mirroring it to create diamonds.

Thicknesses and Fibres

Once you've got the hang of the structure, a great way to deepen your understanding is to try different yarn thicknesses and textures. Threads can behave differently; some are more slippery and others have more grip. With practice you will get to know the characteristics of the different fibres and the varying results they give. Let's take a look at what happens to the scale of the pattern and the feel of the cloth if we change the yarn type.

▲ Shiny cottons, such as this 6-ply, tend to look cleaner and clearer.

▲ Wools are fuzzier, blending and bonding together more.

▲ Chunkier threads such as this thick rug wool will create a larger scale pattern. Thicker threads are definitely quicker to weave, requiring less warp threads and fewer 'overs' and 'unders'.

▲ Thinner, more densely packed threads, such as this fine sewing cotton, will give a smaller-scale pattern. Finer threads will be wrapped many more times around the board and will require many more 'overs' and 'unders' per row. The process takes much longer but is well worth it for the beautiful result.

Chapter 9

Dogtooth

What an odd name for a fabric. Did you know that in French, the name for this pattern, *pied de poule* translates as 'chicken's feet'? In Japan, the name is *chidori*, which is said to refer to a 'flock of birds'. That's my favourite! In the UK, depending on the size of the pattern, we also use the terms 'puppytooth' for small scale and 'houndstooth' for larger scales, though generally, dogtooth and houndstooth are used interchangeably. There are a few variations on the pattern too, but their common defining feature is tessellating shapes in light and dark, created as a result of stripe and structure combined.

You'd be forgiven for assuming that dogtooth has its origins in Scotland, due to its popularity during the 1800s, but early examples of dogtooth fabric have been discovered all over the world. One example was found in Japan dating back to the 1500s, another was found buried in a Swedish peat bog circa 300BCE and another in an Austrian salt mine estimated at 1200BCE.

Although it may look like a very specific design, dogtooth could well have been discovered independently at looms on every continent because it's just a twill and a stripe. I discovered dogtooth by accident in my early weaving days, the instantly recognisable pattern jumping out at me from the loom as I experimented with weaving different structures into a striped warp.

Project 3

Dogtooth

Structure

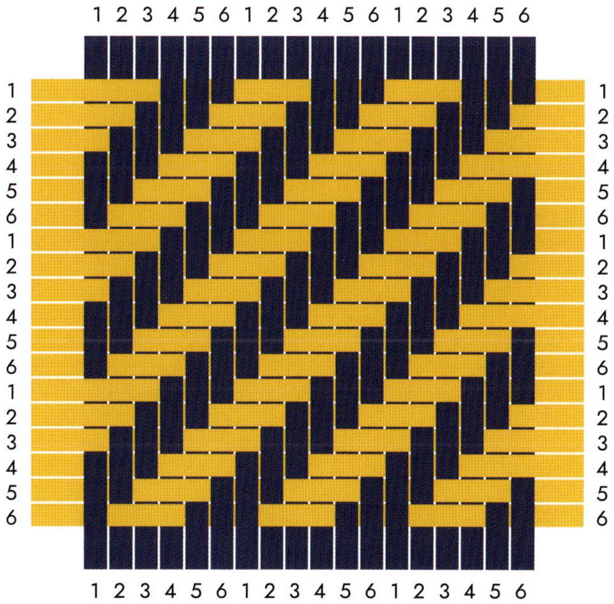

Now you've tried your hand at the 3/3 twill, you can use the same structure to weave a dogtooth. It's just a matter of adding some stripes! The simulation itself doesn't feature the stripes shown in the photo of the weave – it only shows the structure.

You Will Need

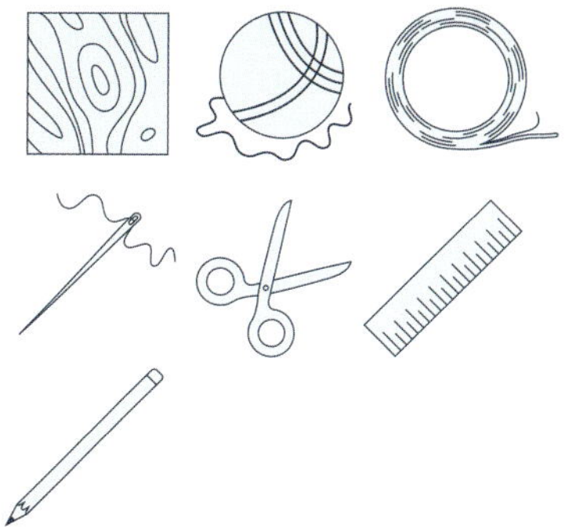

- Square or rectangular wooden base – mine is 10 × 10cm (4 × 4in)
- Yarn in two contrasting colours of the same thickness
- Double-sided adhesive tape
- Flat bodkin or regular sharp needle
- Scissors
- Ruler
- Pencil

Steps

1 Make some marks **on the back** of the board to use as a guide for where to start and stop wrapping your warp threads and where to begin and end weaving. I have marked 2cm (¾in) in from each edge. You can make up your own measurements depending on the size of your base.

2 Lay some strips of double-sided tape longways between the pencil lines. If you would rather not use tape, you can skip this step. Peel a couple of backing strips off on the side you will begin wrapping from.

3 Now you'll wrap your warp threads in **stripes of 6.** Choose your first colour and lay the end down diagonally towards the top marker (if you are left-handed, it'll be the top-left marker). If you're not using tape, just hold the end down with your thumb for the first few wraps.

4 Tie the end of your second colour to the end of your first colour, making sure that the knot will appear on the back of the board.

5 Wrap another 6, and then tie the first colour back on. Keep alternating in stripes of 6 threads, peeling the backing strips as you go.

6 Keep going until you reach the pencil marker. If you need to go over the line a little to complete your stripe, that's fine – you can always manipulate the threads a little so that they fit within the space. It doesn't matter which colour you end on.

7 Secure the end of the thread by tucking it behind the other warp threads on the back. Loop the thread around a few times for extra security (see page 76).

8 Cut a length of weft thread. It doesn't matter which colour you start with. If you want to measure the exact length you'll need, wrap it around the board 6 times and add a little extra to allow for knotting on. Attach the weft using the looping technique.

Weft 1

9 Pass the needle under 3 at the edge, then over 3, under 3, over 3, under 3, all the way across.

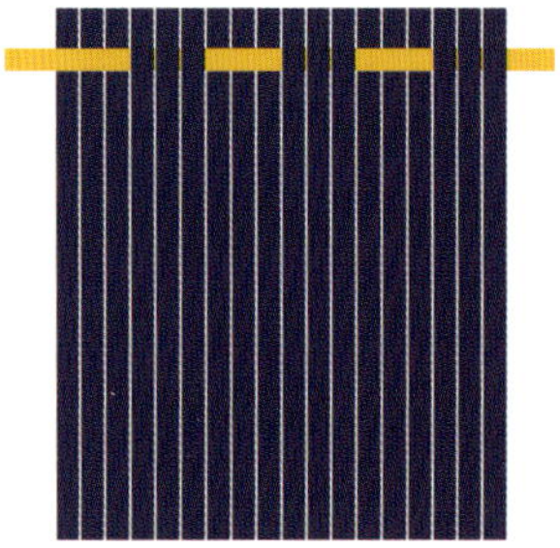

10 This is how your first row will look. Use the needle to straighten it out. Wrap the thread around the back, ready to start your next row.

Tip You can **use the stripes as a reference point** to ensure you are picking up the same sequence of threads with each repeat.

Weft 2

11 Pass the needle **over 1 at the edge**, then under 3, over 3, under 3, over 3, all the way across, ending with over 2.

12 Use your needle to push this row right up to the previous rows. At first, it can feel like this row is repelling the previous row. Once you've woven a bit more, it will become easier to push them together.

Weft 3

13 Pass the needle **over 2 at the edge**, then under 3, over 3, under 3, over 3, all the way across, ending with over 1.

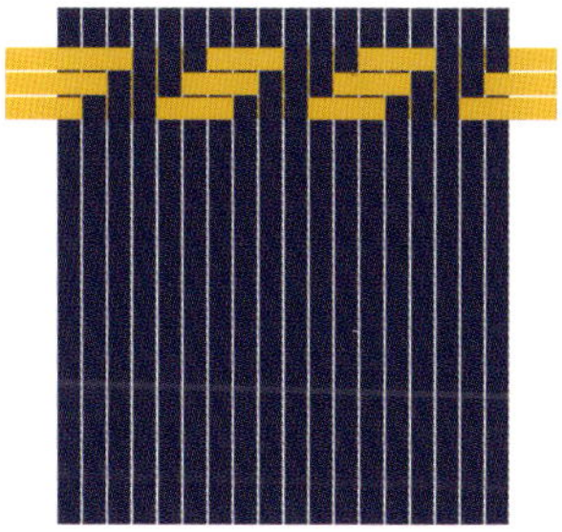

Weft 4

14 Pass the needle over 3 at the edge, then under 3, over 3, under 3, over 3, all the way across, ending with under 3.

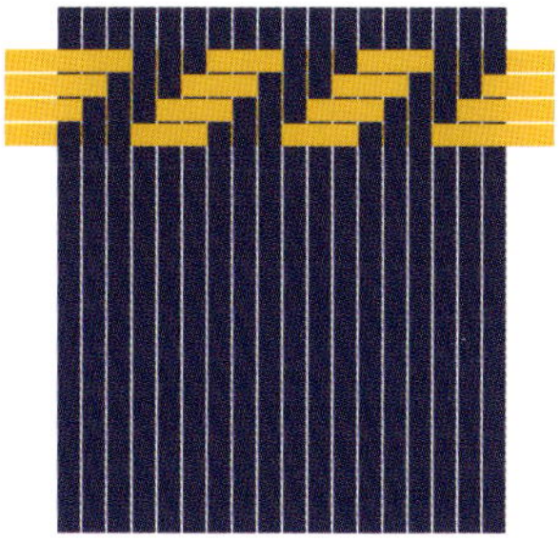

Weft 5

15 Pass the needle **under 1 at the edge**, then over 3, under 3, over 3, under 3, all the way across, ending with under 2.

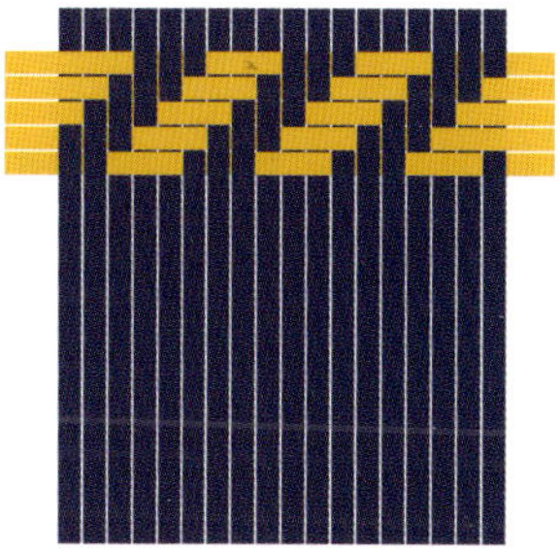

Tip Make sure to push the rows together as much as possible, keeping them straight and compact. Ideally, the threads should be almost as compact as the warp stripes.

Weft 6

16 Pass the needle under 2 at the edge, then over 3, under 3, over 3, under 3, all the way across, ending with under 1.

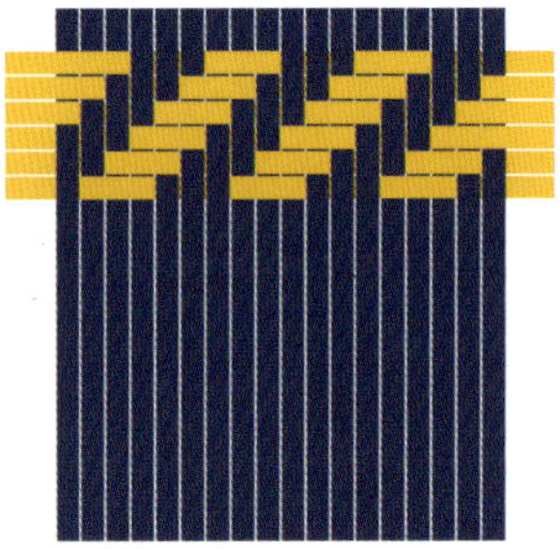

17 That's the first stripe done. Now cut a length of new thread in your second colour and tie the ends together.

18 Repeat the same sequence again but in your second colour. As before, the first row begins again with under 3.

19 Here's how your second stripe will look; this is now one full repeat of the dogtooth pattern.

20 After your third stripe, the pattern should start to jump out at you.

21 That's two full repeats of the dogtooth pattern. Keep repeating this sequence until you reach the finish line.

22 Done! Now it's time to secure the remaining thread.

Tip If you have to go over the line a little to complete your final stripe, don't worry – it won't be noticeable.

23 Pass the thread under a few of the wrapped threads on the **back** of the board, and loop it around a couple of times. Trim any remaining yarn away. Now you can admire your work!

More On Dogtooth

Did you know that you can use other twills to change the scale of your dogtooth? To calculate how many threads you need in each stripe, just add the numbers of the twill together. For example, for the 2/2 twill, its 2 + 2 = 4 threads per stripe (4 dark, 4 light, 4 dark, 4 light). For the 3/3 twill, it's 3 + 3 = 6 threads per stripe (6 dark, 6 light, 6 dark, 6 light). For the 4/4 twill, it's 4 + 4 = 8 threads per stripe; 6/6 = 12 and so on.

▲ A 3/3 twill dogtooth with stripes of 6.

▲ A 2/2 twill dogtooth with stripes of 4.

▲ A 4/4 twill dogtooth with stripes of 8.

▲ A 6/6 twill dogtooth with stripes of 12.

▲ This huge dogtooth has been woven with a 21/21 twill. There are 42 threads in each stripe.

▲ **Top:** Stripes of 8 dark, 8 light, 4/4 twill
Bottom: Stripes of 28 dark, 28 light, 14/14 twill
Here we have two dogtooths of the same scale: one is woven with a thick rug wool and the other with a much finer wool. There are far fewer threads in the thicker version, which makes the pattern look more pixelated. The finer version uses many threads, which gives a much more defined shape.

Gun Club Tweed

Sticking to two colours will give you the most obvious dogtooth pattern because of the contrast between light and dark, but it is possible to create other classic fabrics using the same technique, simply by adding more colours.

▲ Here's an example of a classic gun club tweed. This one is woven with the 2/2 twill, with stripes of 4 threads, only with more colours. Typically, in a gun club check there will be a creamy beige in between each of the other colours. Designs vary in terms of colour order and number, and often there will be a statement brighter colour added in every now and then to create a more visible check.

▲ Traditionally, this fabric was woven using local wool in natural colours to blend in with the rugged landscape, making it the perfect camouflage attire for hunting trips. These days it has become a classic menswear fabric, sure to be found on the Savile Row, and filtering down into the high street.

▲ Here is a comparison between a regular two-colour dogtooth in black and white and a gun club tweed. Both woven in 2/2 twill, both with stripes of 4 threads. In the gun club check, the classic dogtooth shapes are more visible in areas where the darker colours cross over.

Chapter 10

Weave Variations

Now that you understand the dogtooth, you can make many, many other patterns. Don't panic, although these might look complex, they are all in fact woven with the simple twill. It is the variation in stripes combined with the twill that creates the patterns.

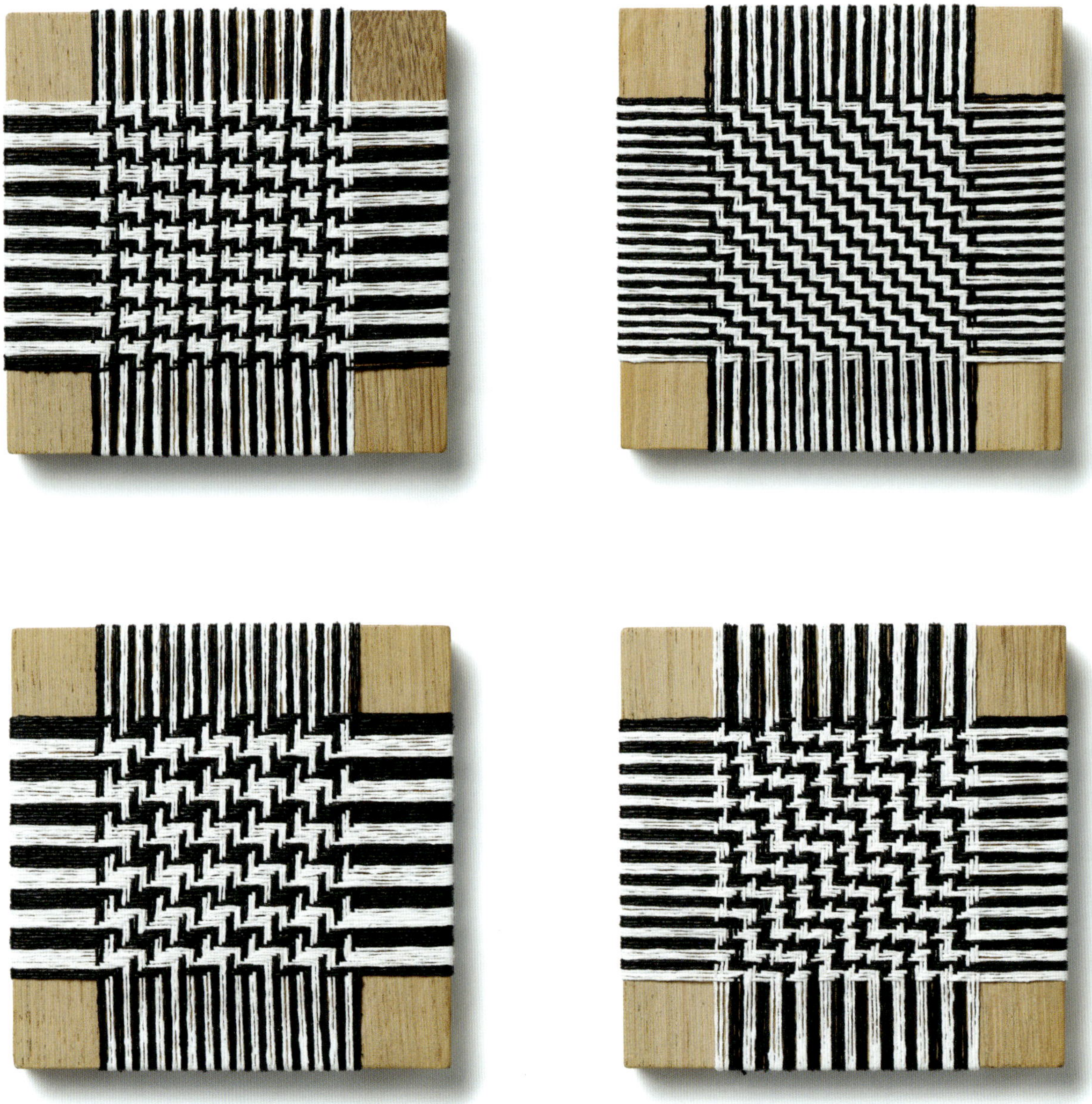

▲ **Top left:** 4/4 twill, warp stripes of 2 black, 2 white, weft stripes of 4 black, 4 white.
Top right: 4/4 twill, warp stripes of 2 black, 2 white, weft stripes of 2 black, 2 white.
Bottom left: 6/6 twill, warp stripes of 2 black, 2 white, weft stripes of 6 black, 6 white.
Bottom right: 4/4 twill, warp stripes of 3 black, 3 white, weft stripes of 3 black, 3 white.

▲ **Top left:** 4/4 twill, warp stripes of 4 black, 4 white, weft stripes of 4 black, 4 white.
Top right: 6/6 twill, warp stripes of 6 black, 6 white, weft stripes of 3 black, 3 white.
Bottom left: 6/6 twill, warp stripes of 2 black, 2 white, weft stripes of 4 black, 4 white.
Bottom right: 4/4 twill, warp stripes of 6 black, 6 white, weft stripes of 6 black, 6 white.

The Versatility of Warp Stripes

When weaving at the loom, a long striped warp can sometimes feel a little limiting. But actually there is bags of potential for pattern in a stripe. It can be fun to use a slightly longer base and see how many different patterns you can make using the same warp stripes. Here are some examples of twill, hopsack and waffle structures, showing their versatility.

Top left (Warp stripes 1 & 1)
Top weave: 3/3 twill, weft stripes of 3 black, 3 white. **Middle weave:** 6/6 twill, weft stripes of 1 black, 1 white. **Bottom weave:** 3/3 twill, weft stripes of 2 black, 2 white.

Top right (Warp stripes 2 & 2)
Top weave: 4/4 twill, weft stripes of 2 black, 2 white. **Middle weave:** 4/4 twill, weft stripes of 4 black, 4 white. **Bottom weave:** 2/2 twill, weft stripes of 1 black, 1 white.

Bottom left (Warp stripes 4 & 4)
Top weave: 2/2 twill, weft stripes of 4 black, 4 white. **Middle weave:** 2/2 hopsack, weft stripes of 4 black, 4 white. **Bottom weave:** 4/4 twill, weft stripes of 4 black, 4 white.

Bottom right (Warp stripes 6 & 6)
Top weave: 3/3 twill, weft stripes of 6 black, 6 white. **Middle weave:** Waffle, weft stripes of 6 black, 6 white. **Bottom weave:** 6/6 twill, weft stripes of 3 black, 3 white.

Tweed

Traditionally, tweed was woven from the wool of local sheep, particularly in regions such as Scotland, Ireland, and northern England. Each flock produced their own quality; some soft, some coarse. The wool would be spun and woven in its wide spectrum of undyed shades, or dyed with plants, lichens and roots, reflecting the palette of the rugged landscape.

Most tweed fabrics are woven in a twill structure, often in variations such as herringbone or broken twill. Woven in wool, the structure produces a strong, durable cloth that is naturally water-resistant.

Some say the name 'tweed' was a happy accident, born from a misspelling in a letter or invoice in the 1830s about a shipment of cloth. The Scots word for twill was 'tweel', but the merchant misread it as 'tweed', assuming it referred to the River Tweed, which runs across the Scottish Borders into northern England. And the name stuck.

In the nineteenth century, tweed became a favourite for the British aristocracy, especially for country sports like hunting, shooting and fishing. Over time, the style filtered down to wider society, boosting production and earning the fabric global recognition.

One of the most well known tweed makers is Harris Tweed, which is so celebrated in the UK that an act of parliament has been passed to protect it. The Harris Tweed Act of 1993 ensures that genuine Harris Tweed is handwoven at home in the Outer Hebrides, using locally spun and dyed wool. Every piece stamped with the Orb symbol is a guarantee of authenticity, origin and quality. It's a rare example of legislation that directly protects a traditional craft and its makers.

Herringbone

The herringbone pattern is also a twill. The twill changes direction every now and then, a bit like a zigzag, but there is a 'shift' before the direction change, and the bands of twill are vertical rather than horizontal.

▲ If you want to try weaving the herringbone, wrap your warp widthways around your board…

▲ …And weave into it longways. This makes the structure much easier to follow.

▶ Take a look at the 'shift' between sections. When you change direction, first weave a row that is the complete opposite of the previous one then implement your direction change.

Simulations

▲ Traditional herringbone structure with vertical bands.

▲ Turning the structure around to better suit the process of off-loom weaving, making each row easier to follow. You can decide how many threads are in each band before your direction change. Some herringbones are quite widely spaced; others are narrow.

Extra Herringbone Options

▲ Why not try adding in a couple of contrasting threads to make a check?

▲ Or weaving a different colour with every band?

Chapter 11

Colour

When I teach, I'm always intrigued by the variety of colour palettes that emerge across the tables throughout the day. Unexpected pairings I might never have thought to put together, yet they work so beautifully. As Josef Albers expresses in *Interactions of Colour*, 'Everyone has preference for certain colours and prejudices against others.'

A couple of years ago I started offering attendees of my online classes the opportunity to choose their own colour palettes for their starter kits. Some requested earth tones, others wanted high-saturation bright tones. Some asked for just neutrals, others only blues and greens. Some used mood words to describe their preferences: a 'gentle' palette, or a 'playful' one. On more than one occasion I've had requests for colours that 'clash', which I love.

Given the opportunity, almost everyone takes up the offer to pick their own colours, but on the odd occasion (and quite bravely), someone might ask for a 'lucky dip'. Surprisingly often, people say things like 'anything is fine but absolutely no orange please', and then the next person will ask specifically for orange. The same with pastels.

Colour Taste

Despite many of us absorbing influences from similar sources; pop culture, trends in fashion, art and design, we *still* all manage to develop our own individual tastes when it comes to colour. This, along with my own explorations into colour, has given rise to many questions on the topic of taste:

- Why do we like the colours we do?
- What gives us our individual preferences in colour, and why do one person's differ from another's?
- Do our preferences evolve as we make our way through life?
- What does it mean to have a 'good eye' for colour?
- How can a single colour draw some people in and make others move away?
- Is there such a thing as social etiquette when it comes to colours? An appropriate time and place for purple, a particular moment for orange?

For me, certain groupings of colours can really sing. It is a physical response. Just the right amount of one colour next to a perfect slice of another, followed by a flash of something unexpected, can really set something off in my brain. When I stumble upon a harmonious combination I experience a feeling of growing excitement, an inspired feeling of positivity.

Sometimes, it is enough just to appreciate the beauty of a pleasing colour pairing without thoughts of possible applications. Not all colour experiences need to be imagined as a garment or a home textile. Thoughts of their potential for use in design seem almost to take away from their validity to exist just as they are.

My Research on Colour Preferences

As part of the research for this chapter, I asked others for their thoughts and experiences on colour. Their responses were insightful and varied. Some expressed great excitement at being asked, for it had never occurred to them to question their natural inclinations on colour before. It turns out that some people experience colour not just with their eyes but with other senses too. Some can smell, taste or even hear colours. Many told me that they 'feel' colours in a visceral way. Some explained that, for them, colour is a source of energy. One participant shared that she had begun to experience colour entirely differently after a brain injury. Another told me that she sees colour combinations when she is dropping off to sleep at night.

In the same way that some colour pairings can light us up, others can switch us right off. Many felt they couldn't express their aversion with words, they only had a feeling. Those who could articulate it described the sensation as 'jarring', or 'unsettling'. One explained that certain colour pairings could really 'set their teeth on edge'. I've experienced this in my own weaving, having added in a colour that I usually love, only for its presence to completely throw the rest of the palette off.

Some expressed a desire to be more adventurous with colour. Many people told me that there is a clear distinction between the colours they wear and those they choose to work with. However, I can't tell you how many times I have seen people subconsciously choosing to work with colours that match their outfit or nail colour.

Colour and Design Sensitivities

We develop our colour and design sensibilities from a melting pot of lived experience; culture, countless external influences and cognitive associations. This is not a conscious effort – we are continually taking in visual information. We're seeing, experiencing, processing and building our preferences all the time.

Cultural colour 'meanings' can be deeply ingrained, yet they often vary widely between different parts of the world. Personal experiences – whether positive or negative – can influence how we respond to certain colours, fabrics, styles or even textures. We attach memories to sensory experiences, often linking them to specific emotions, which is why colour is such a powerful marketing tool.

Our tastes can change, too, as we make our way through life. As we learn new things, absorb new cultures and have new experiences, we might find ourselves leaning into a new palette. We might love a colour at some point, and go off it at another, but it is our perception that changes, not the object, colour or material.

Colour in Context

Colours interact with one another in all sorts of unexpected ways, presenting their characteristics differently depending on their surroundings. When placed side by side, they have the power to bring out each other's best qualities or dull them down.

We rarely experience colours in isolation. How a colour looks to us depends on the context it appears in. On a yarn shade card, individual colours are often surrounded by a white border, which, while practical, can make it difficult to visualise how colours might work together. How a colour looks on its own can be quite different to how it looks side by side with another colour. As part of a larger palette, its identity changes again.

Sometimes a colour pairing that would normally be your very last choice becomes the perfect one in the context of a specific palette. In *Interaction of Colour*, Josef Albers uses the term 'colour relativity' to describe the way that colours behave together. Albers often compares colour pairings or groupings to human relationships and roles, referring to them as 'parent' colours, 'siblings' or 'actors in a cast', performing for an audience, demanding an emotional response.

When we listen to music, we perceive each sound as part of a larger whole. Some instruments play a supporting role, others lead, but every element contributes to the overall effect of the piece. It's the same with colour. Sometimes, the tiniest slither of what you might think of as an 'ordinary' colour can bring an entire palette to life.

The Formula for Balance

There are no bad colours. I would even venture to say that there are no bad colour combinations – it's just a case of finding a pleasing balance of proportions that is restful to look at. As we go through our lives, we learn to recognise visual harmony. We instinctively respond positively when we experience a balanced composition. We may not feel well practised at creating one from scratch, but we know it when we see it. We also can recognise when something doesn't look quite right.

Whether you're working with two colours or twenty, the same basic principles (not rules!) can be followed to create harmony. It's all about proportions, quantity, placement and tone.

Think about the concept of 'main colours' and 'accent' or 'highlight' colours. This is often referred to as 'colour ratios'. A 'main' colour, also described as the 'ground', 'base' or 'dominant' colour, is the one that is used in the largest amounts and can be seen most visibly from a distance. A 'highlight', or 'accent' colour can be used in smaller amounts to add a flash of zing to your palette or break up the more dominant colours a little. A tiny amount can have a surprisingly big impact.

Sometimes, putting a load of brights together can have a dulling effect. If you love bright colours, consider using neutrals or muted colour tones in between. This provides a little separation between the brighter colours, making them pop more. Some colours play supportive roles, helping to bring out other colours to their full potential. Every colour in your palette has a vital part to play. Sometimes that is not clear until the piece is finished. Adding a large area of a 'plain' colour can feel underwhelming at the time, but its presence can really set off the other colours beautifully.

You don't have to use all the colours of the rainbow at once to make an exciting composition. Even exploring the many tints and tones within one single colour family – green, for example – can offer a world of possibilities. Within one colour grouping there will be an arrangement to make them look loud, another to quiet them. This can be done by switching up their quantities or swapping their order.

▲ Here, I've arranged the colours so that there are balanced quantities of lights, darks, muted colours and brights across an arrangement of narrow and wide stripes.

Intuition

If you are fearful of your abilities to choose a good colour palette because you haven't studied colour theory, allow me to put your mind at rest.

Many people swear by the colour wheel, and many weavers use the Fibonacci sequence to achieve balance in their stripe proportions. Some designers use percentages, like Jessica Sowerby, who champions the '70%, 20%, 10% & a Dash' rule in her book, *Colour Confidence*. For me, the colour wheel feels like a more technical or academic approach to colour. It's good to have it there 'just in case', but it's important not to let a specific formula influence or guide you away from a pairing that excites you. It is true that colours that sit opposite each other on the colour wheel are naturally harmonious, but there are plenty of other combinations that work beautifully together if their saturation or value is adjusted. Rather than the colours themselves, often it is tonality and proportion that determines whether a palette feels harmonious or discordant.

My advice is to refer to colour theory as a secondary resource as and when needed, so as not to drown out your own intuition, which is by far your most powerful tool. Our initial instincts are often surprisingly accurate and a good indicator of how we feel and what we are drawn to. Whichever method you choose, all are valid – there is no wrong way to go about choosing colours. The colours are right when you feel they are.

Designing a Palette

Choosing a palette from scratch can be daunting, especially if we are presented with multiple options. Sometimes, we might have a clear idea right from the start about the colours we would like to use, while at other times we can feel totally stumped. You don't have to pick out your whole palette before starting a piece. In fact, the less attached you are to the end result the better.

If you're struggling, just start with a colour you like and build slowly from there. This first colour may turn out to play only a minor role in the palette, or it could be the main feature. Often, as you begin to place colours side by side, unexpected things begin to happen. I highly recommend asking others for their opinion on which colour comes next. Even if you don't agree with their suggestion, this can still be helpful. Establishing which colours we don't want to use can help us on the path to choosing the ones we do.

When it comes to choosing a second or third colour, there is something to be said for intuitive choices, made on a whim. It might be that you only add a tiny stripe of something before choosing a third colour, or perhaps two colours is enough. Wrap your chosen colour until you are happy with the amount, then try holding up various colour options next to it to see if anything jumps out. If you decide to stick to two colours, it can be fun to play with stripe proportions. You might like to explore a random, irregular composition or a more regimented, orderly arrangement of stripes.

As you make your way through your composition it can be useful to stand back and consider the palette as a whole, judging the overall balance. Each time we add a new colour, the whole palette will change. Sometimes the addition of a tiny slither of something at the end can set the whole thing off. If you'd like to add a colour but you're afraid it might overpower the rest of the palette, use it sparingly.

It can be difficult to visualise how two colours are going to look once they're woven together. Keep an open mind – it's all about exploring and testing things out at the beginning. It can be easy to add too many colours to a palette, especially if you're having doubts about your choices thus far and you want to try to 'rescue' it. Have faith, and try not to overthink it. It is easy to talk yourself out of a great colour choice.

Yarn Windings

If you do want to have your colours and stripe proportions decided before you begin, small yarn wrappings are a great way to develop a palette. Practising on a piece of card takes the pressure off getting it right first time on the real thing. Many weavers make wrappings to test out compositions and layouts or to map out their stripes when planning large warps. This method is applicable across many design fields besides weaving.

Colour Mixing in Weaving

The way that colours mix together when woven varies depending on fibre, thickness, density and structure. You may feel limited by your available materials, but there are many ways to use what you have to produce a wide range of results.

Is your thread shiny or matte? Hairy or smooth? Does it reflect light? How thick is the yarn? How densely packed are your warp threads? What kind of structure are you using? By playing with these variables we can manipulate light and shading, stretching the limitations of our palette.

▶ It can be useful to practise weaving a variety of colour pairings to create a library of references.

Magic Tricks

I used to think that mixing colours in weaving was like mixing paint, but a red warp and a yellow weft don't always make an orange fabric. The more I experiment, the more I realise that weaving holds its own magic and depth – its own science – when it comes to colour.

A little like Impressionist paintings or Lichtenstein's dots, sometimes it can be possible to create the 'effect' of a third colour (besides that of warp and weft), especially when viewed from a distance.

In some of his colour experiments, Josef Albers used paper, not paint, to 'mix' colours, or at least to create the illusion that a mixture is being viewed. Like Albers's papers, woven structure can perform magic tricks, making your eyes mix the colours instead.

Fibre

Texture matters. A colour can have a totally different impact depending on its material. The same colour in glass, plastic, wood, metal, paper or textile will present differently as it interacts with light.

As such, a cloth woven in wool will show its colours differently to one woven in silk. The hairiness of the wool will make for a painterly, blended effect, whereas smooth fibres like silk, viscose or mercerised cotton can appear more vibrant. A matte yarn, though less vibrant, will show its truer colour, whereas a shiny one will reflect light, making the colour appear changeable depending on the angle from which it is viewed.

The thicker the yarn, the more visible the woven structure will be and, in turn, the more separated the warp and weft colours will look. Thin threads, however, that are more densely packed together, can appear to blend the colours more seamlessly.

If the thread count of your warp is the same as that of your weft, the colours in each will be equally balanced. If the warp threads are more densely packed than the weft, the warp colour will be dominant.

The Power of a Warp

I think every weaver has had the (frustrating) experience of believing they have found the perfect colour, only to discover that, once woven, its appearance has changed, its vibrance diluted by the dominance of the warp colour.

The only ways we can achieve a solid colour result in weaving are when the warp and weft are the same colour, or if we are using a 'warp-faced' or 'weft-faced' structure. Sometimes, if there is a difference in thickness between the warp and the weft yarn, it can be possible to produce varying levels of coverage.

Using White and Black

A white warp can lift some colours and dilute others. Black can be surprisingly powerful as a base colour. On a black background, pale colours can appear almost white; equally, on a white background, dark colours can appear almost black.

You don't have to use pure white and pure black to add light or darkness to a palette. Sometimes, I find that they break up a palette too much. However, there are many instances when the addition of white can really bring out some of the very lightest tints of other colours. Try using 'almost blacks' and 'almost whites' – colours with a lot of black added, like dark green, burgundy or teal, or a lot of white added, like a very pale green, peach or latte.

Interestingly, white can be used as a palette cleanser for the eyes. If you are feeling overwhelmed from looking at colours, try looking at a white sheet of paper for a few moments, and allow your eyes to rest.

▲ This piece is woven with shiny cotton embroidery floss, but if a hairy, matte wool was used, the results would be different again.

Using Structure to Create Light and Shade

Choosing the right woven structure can help us to create 'shades' within the mixing of two colours.

A 'twill' structure will display colour differently to, say, a 'hopsack' or a 'satin'. Further to that, structures can be adjusted to show varying degrees of balance between warp and weft.

A 'warp-facing' structure will show more of the warp colour on the front of the fabric, hiding the majority of the wefts on the reverse, and a 'weft-facing' structure will show more of the weft colour on the front, the warp threads hidden on the underside.

In the case of the 3/3 twill, the weft passes 'over 3 and under 3' – an equal balance between warp and weft. Other structures will show, for example, 3 warp threads for every 1 weft thread, or vice versa, resulting in an imbalance of colour distribution.

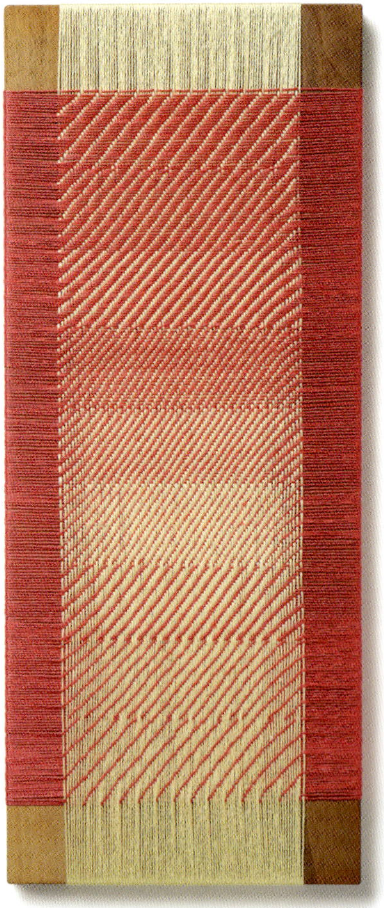

▶The 3/1 twill (over 3, under 1, over 3, under 1 and so on) is weft dominant, whereas the 1/7 twill (over 1, under 7, over 1, under 7) shows more of the warp.

Limitations

There are millions of colours, but when working with yarn, we are often limited to a fairly narrow choice. If you're not a dyer yourself, it can be difficult to get hold of that perfect hue. Shop-bought yarn may come in a limited number of shades and if, like me, you prefer working with second-hand or industry-waste yarn, you must make do with what is available at the time.

Losing access to my loom and yarn stash forced me to find other ways to weave, using whatever thread I could find around the house. Sometimes limitations can sharpen our experience, giving us an opportunity to utilise our problem-solving skills.

To take this a step further, it can be fun to impose limitations on purpose. For example, choosing to use only one fibre type, eliminating all others, but exploring all the variables within that range. Or perhaps selecting just one structure and comparing the results when woven with different types of thread. It is amazing how many variations are achievable within quite strict boundaries. Each fibre type behaves differently.

Why not try focusing on one colour or a single colour family? What happens when you combine a smooth, shiny green with a matte, hairy green? For me, twill is one of the most versatile structures – it can create many different patterns when used in combination with colour and stripe. But sticking to one solid colour, seeing the structure in its most basic and naked form, highlights its character and nuances, showing its beauty in a way that can sometimes become a little diluted once colour and stripe come into play.

▲ Here, I chose to impose two limitations, using only white and only twill. By doing this I discovered just how many whites there are, and that the twill structure is incredibly beautiful in the absence of colour.

Chapter 12

Check

A 'check' or 'plaid' is usually woven using a simple structure such as twill, 'plain weave' (over 1, under 1) or hopsack. The pattern is created as a result of stripes in both the warp and the weft.

A check can be just two colours or multiple colours. The stripes can be regular, or random in their placement. Sometimes the colours in warp and weft are matching, sometimes they are different.

The scale of the check can be tiny, like a small-scale grid, or huge. Some check designs repeat across the fabric, while others don't.

Project 4

Check

Structure

Now we are going to make a check, and – you guessed it – we are going to use our old faithful 3/3 twill again, this time in combination with colour stripes of various proportions to create a unique check design.

You Will Need

- Base – mine is 12 × 18cm (4¾ × 8in)
- Yarn – I am using various shiny cotton embroidery floss, approximately 6–8 ply
- Regular sharp needle
- Scissors
- Double-sided adhesive tape
- Ruler
- Pencil

Steps

1 Prepare your base for weaving by marking out your guidelines. If you want to map out the dimensions of your stripes before wrapping, make some pencil marks on the back to use as a guide. This works well if you want all of your stripes to be the same size, to fit evenly between your main markers. If you're planning to decide as you go along (like me!), there is no need to make extra marks.

2 Tape the back of the board (optional). Peel a couple of strips off on the side that you will begin wrapping from.

3 I am going to demonstrate the 'make it up as you go' approach to choosing colours. I've simply started with a colour I like. Start wrapping the thread around the board, laying each thread side by side, one after the other. When you feel you've wound enough of your first colour, stop. Cut the thread, leaving enough length to comfortably tie the next colour to the end.

4 Choose a colour that you feel sits well with your first. Wrap as much as you like of this colour.

5 Think about stripe proportions as you go – but don't overthink it. I am going for random stripe proportions here so I'm going to vary the sizes, which can also help to balance the colours. Add as many stripes and colours as you like.

6 If you're unsure on your final colour, stand back and look at the stripes from the front. What does the palette need to create balance?

Tip Don't get too attached to the warp stripes; and equally don't worry if you're feeling unsure about your choices because the weaving process will change the overall appearance quite drastically.

7 Now that you have wound your warp, you need to secure the end of the thread. Pass the needle under a few wrapped threads on the back. Pull the needle through. Make some loops, then trim away any excess thread.

8 Think about which colour you'd like to weave your weft with first. Are you matching your weft colours to your warp colours or going for something new? Cut a length of yarn and thread the needle at one end. Attach the end of the weft thread to the wrapped warp threads on the back of the board using the looping technique.

Weft 1

9 Pass the needle **under 3 at the very edge**, then over 3, under 3, over 3, under 3, all the way across.

10 Bit by bit, make your way across to the other side, continuing your 'over 3, under 3, over 3, under 3' sequence.

Tip This thread is thinner than the wool and the shiny cotton is more slippery, so take extra care as you go and keep an eye on warp threads sliding behind each other.

11 This is how your first row will look. When you're satisfied, wrap the remaining thread around the back, and around to the front to begin weft 2.

Weft 2

12 Pass the needle **over 1 at the very edge**, then under 3, over 3, under 3, over 3, all the way across.

13 Use your needle to push the rows as close together as possible.

Weft 3

14 Pass the needle **over 2 at the very edge**, then under 3, over 3, under 3, over 3, all the way across.

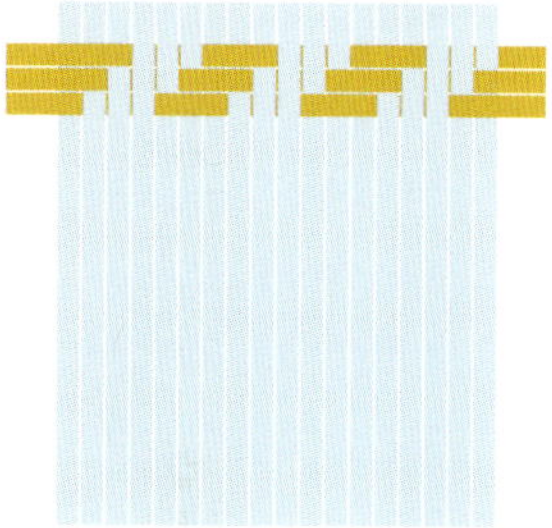

Weft 4

15 Pass the needle **over 3 at the very edge**, then under 3, over 3, under 3, over 3, all the way across.

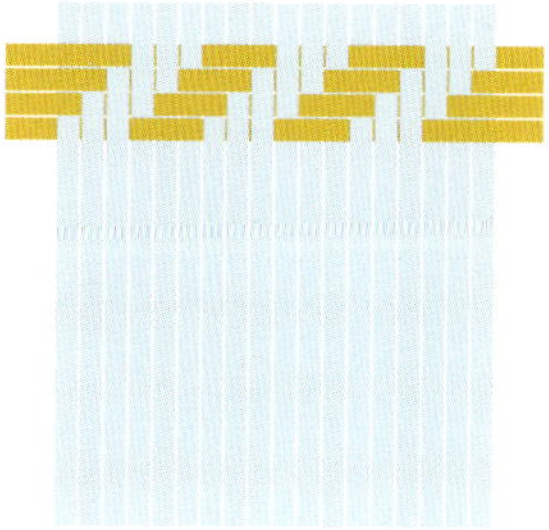

Weft 5

16 Pass the needle **under 1 at the very edge**, then over 3, under 3, over 3, under 3, all the way across.

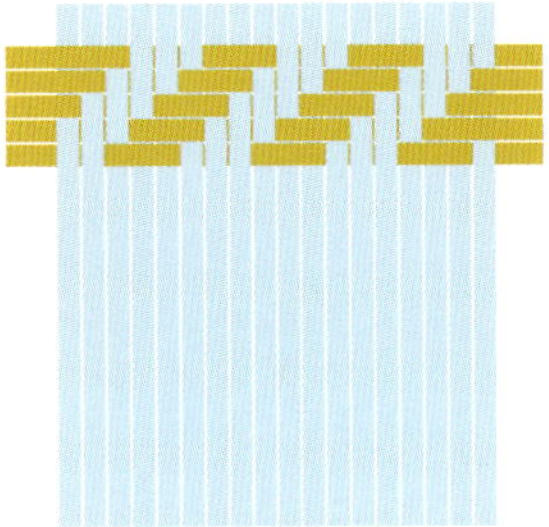

Weft 6

17 Pass the needle **under 2 at the very edge**, then over 3, under 3, over 3, under 3, all the way across.

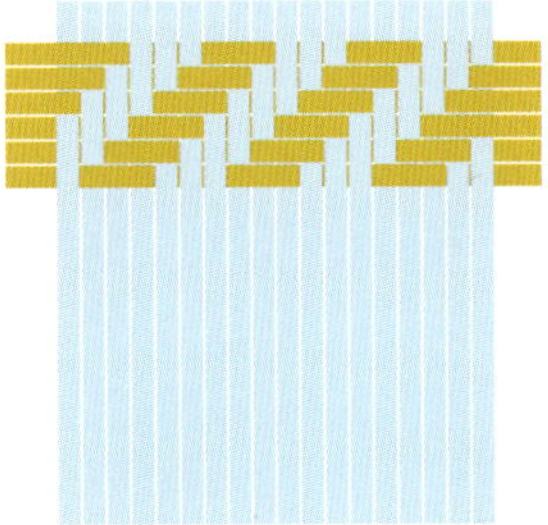

18 That's one whole sequence of the 3/3 twill structure complete. To continue the pattern, begin again from weft 1 and repeat the whole sequence.

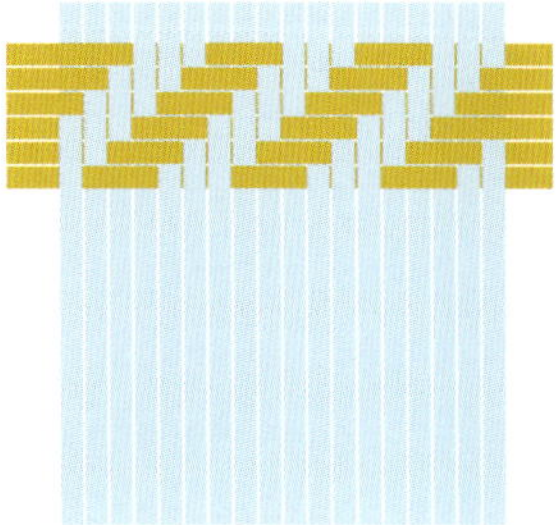

19 Keep going until you feel you have woven enough in that colour. To decide which colour to go for next, it can be helpful to hold them up to the board to see which one feels right. Remember, you can change colour whenever you want to – you don't have to wait until you've completed a structural repeat.

Tip It is important not to stress too much about whether you're choosing well – every time you add a new colour, the look of the weave will change completely. Just go with it.

20 Tie a knot to attach your next colour. Continue with your second colour until you're ready for another change.

21 Keep adding more stripes, standing back from time to time to assess the colour balance.

22 I finish with a burgundy to balance light and dark in the check. Notice how the addition of weft stripes has totally changed the look of the piece since you were looking at just the warp stripes, pre-weaving. What I love about the 'make it up as you go' approach is that you never know how the check will turn out, and there are many opportunities along the way to change the direction it's headed in.

23 Secure the remaining thread on the back of the board using the looping technique. Trim any remaining yarn away.

Extras To Try

Why not experiment by weaving your check in an unusual yarn. This one is woven in mohair, which can be brushed afterwards to achieve a blended painterly look.

Opposite are some examples firstly showing just the warp, and then what the check looks like once the weft stripes are woven in.

▲ A large scale Gingham woven in mohair, brushed.

▲ Two colours, regularly proportioned stripes, warp and weft colours matching.

▲Multicolour, warp stripes narrower than weft stripes, warp and weft colours matching.

▲ Multicolour, regularly proportioned stripes, warp and weft colours matching.

▲ Multicolour, irregularly proportioned stripes, warp and weft colours matching.

▲ Regularly proportioned stripes in various tones and shades of purple, warp and weft colours matching.

▲ Four colours, regularly proportioned stripes, warp and weft colours matching.

Chapter 13

Pattern Discovery

▶ This gradient check is woven in the simple 3/3 twill all the way through. The stripes in the warp and the weft consist of two shades of green – a light and a dark – ordered in a gradient from one to the other.

Sometimes, the 'up-close' nature of off-loom weaving can lead to all sorts of discoveries. Following on from **Weave Variations** (see page 102), these next patterns are simply a result of the combination of **stripe and twill**.

A gradient is created when the warp and weft stripes are carefully ordered to form a subtle ombre from one colour to another, as opposed to solid blocks of colour.

As a fabric, when viewed on a larger scale and from a distance, the gradient check can create an optical illusion; areas of check begin to appear as rounded orbs of colour. But, up close, the fabric offers something entirely different – a fascinating array of small-scale patterns – something I myself did not appreciate until weaving off-loom with needle and thread.

If you'd like to try this check, take a look at the colour order of the threads in the simulation (the same for both warp and weft). I've used a fine 2/10Nm wool (approx. 28 threads per inch). It is woven with a 3/3 twill.

The gradient from one colour to another gives us various groupings of stripes to study, making it a great exercise for discovery. Let's take a closer look. How many different patterns could be hiding here?

All of the following examples show patterns that appear somewhere in the gradient check. You could be forgiven for imagining that each pattern must have a different construction, but they really are all woven in 3/3 twill. It is the colour order of the threads that create the patterns.

▶ **Top left:** Warp = 2 light, 2 dark. Weft = 2 light, 2 dark.

Top right: Warp = 4 light, 1 dark. Weft = 4 light, 1 dark.

Bottom left: Warp = 5 light, 1 dark. Weft = 1 dark, 2 light.

Bottom right: Warp = 3 light, 1 dark. Weft = all light.

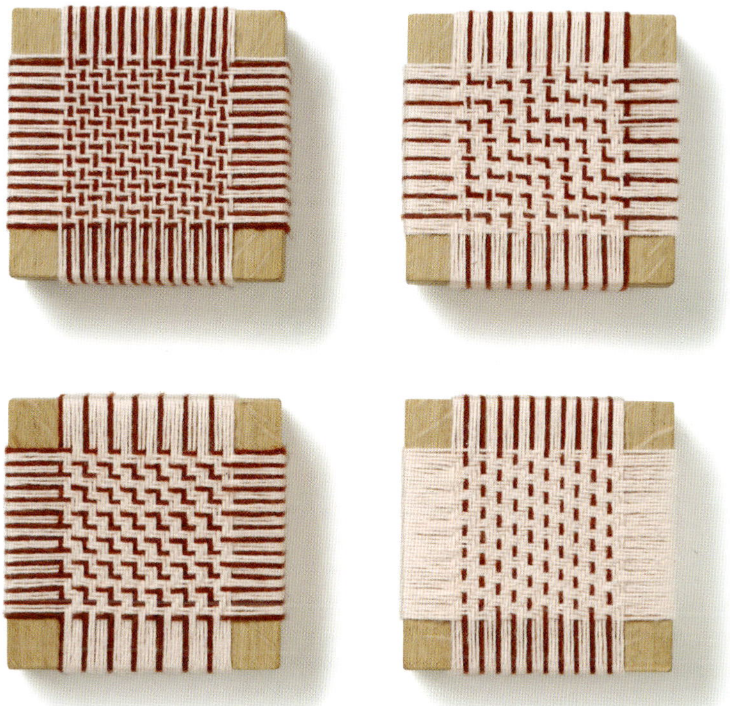

▶ **Top left:** Warp = 1 dark, 2 light. Weft = 2 dark, 1 light.

Top right: Warp = 1 light, 5 dark. Weft = 1 light, 5 dark.

Bottom left: Warp = 1 light, 5 dark. Weft = 1 light, 5 dark (different starting point).

Bottom right: Warp = 1 light, 2 dark. Weft = 1 light, 2 dark.

Project 5

Hopsack

If the twill felt a little brain-twisting, you'll be delighted to know that there is a structure that is much simpler but just as versatile. The name 'hopsack' originates from its initial use as woven sack material used to transport hops from the farm to the brewery.

Structure

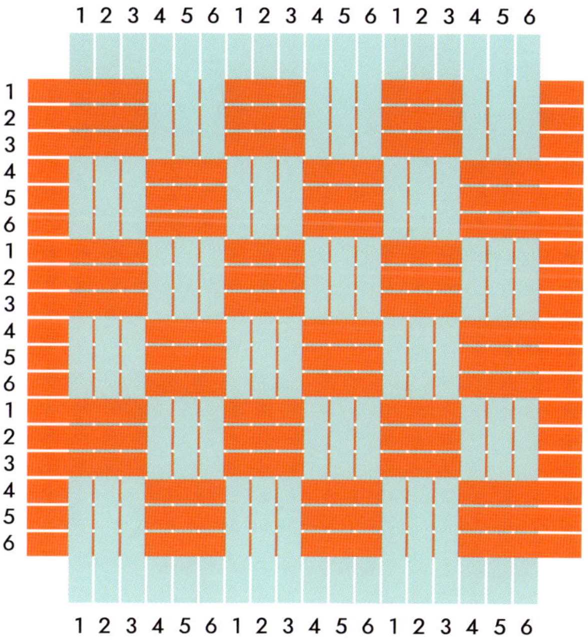

This is the simulation we'll be working from to create our hopsack.

- The pattern repeats every 6 threads.
- This structure creates a chequerboard effect by repeating the same row three times and then switching to the opposite three times.
- This is a 3 × 3 hopsack, but you can also weave 4 × 4 and any other number.
- The simulation can be read from right to left, or from left to right, depending on your handedness.

You Will Need

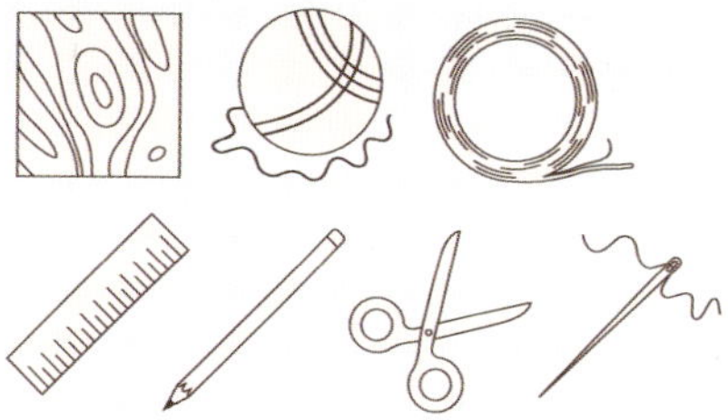

- Square or rectangle base – mine is 7 × 15cm (2¾ × 6in)
- Yarn – I have used 4-ply wool
- Double-sided adhesive tape
- Ruler
- Pencil
- Scissors
- Flat bodkin or regular sharp needle

Steps

1 Decide where you'd like to begin wrapping. Make marks on the back of your base with a pencil and ruler to use as a guide. If it helps, you can draw a line to connect the marks.

2 Lay some strips of double-sided tape on the back (this is optional). Peel a couple of strips away from the side you'll begin wrapping from.

3 Lay the end down diagonally towards your starting point. If you are left-handed, you will begin from the left.

4 It can be helpful to **wrap your warp threads in threes** for this structure.

5 Peel off the backing strips as you go and stop when you reach your marker.

6 Cut the thread but leave enough length to thread the needle. Pass the needle under some of the wrapped threads on the **back**. Pull the thread through.

7 Make some loops to secure the thread and trim any excess away.

8 Choose a contrasting colour for your weft. Cut roughly 1m (39in) of yarn, and thread the needle. Attach the end of the thread to the back of the board, using the looping technique. Turn your board over and get ready to start weaving.

Weft 1

9 Pass the needle under 3 then over 3, and repeat all the way across. Take it bit by bit – no need to weave all the way across in one go.

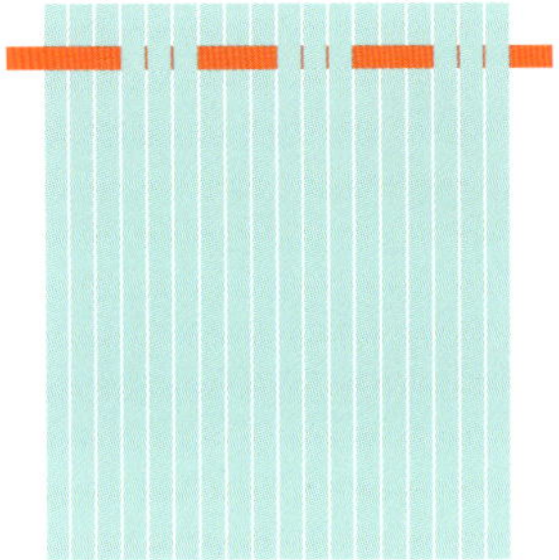

10 Here's how your first row should look. Wrap the remaining thread around the back, and back around to the front to begin your second row.

Weft 2

11 Now repeat the exact same row again...

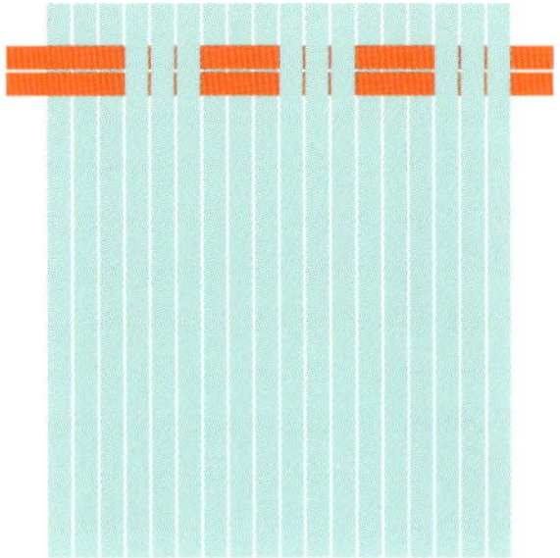

Weft 3

12 ...And again.

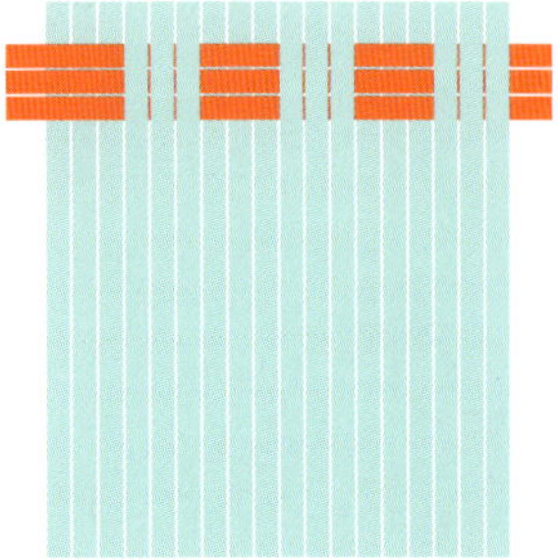

Weft 4

13 Now do the opposite. Wherever you went **over** before, now go under, and wherever you went **under** before, now go over.

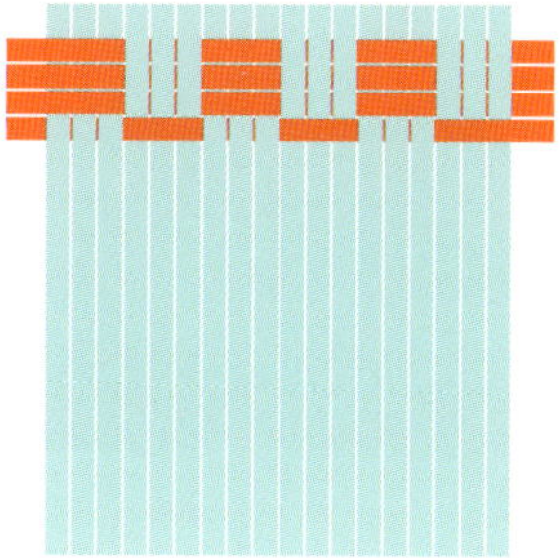

14 Use the needle to compact the wefts as much as you can. If you run out of thread, just tie on a new length, making sure the knot appears on the back.

Wefts 5–6

15 Repeat this twice more so that you have three of the same weft.

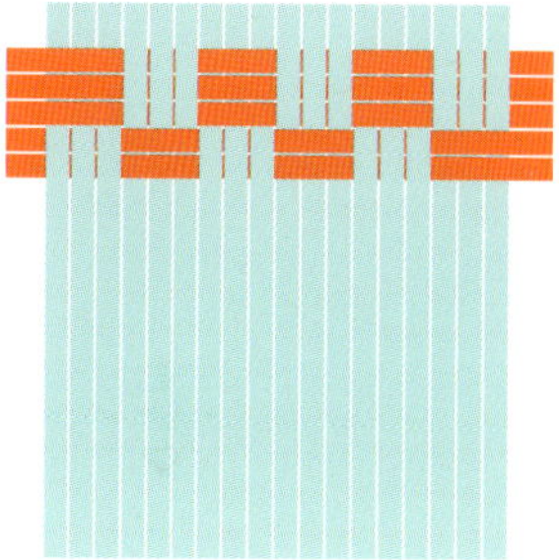

16 Now begin at weft 1 again.

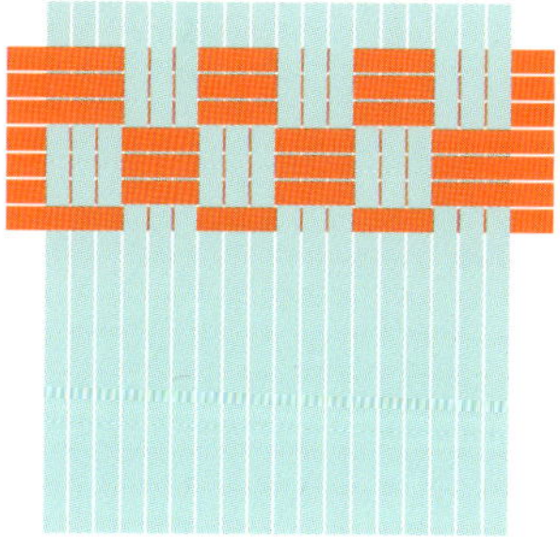

17 This is what one full sequence looks like – now just repeat the whole thing again and again until you reach the finish line.

18 This is what two repeats looks like.

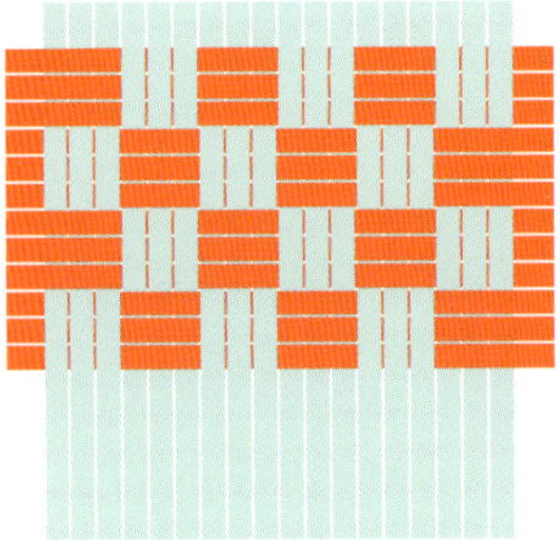

19 Here's the finished piece. Now secure the last thread on the back of the board, using the looping technique.

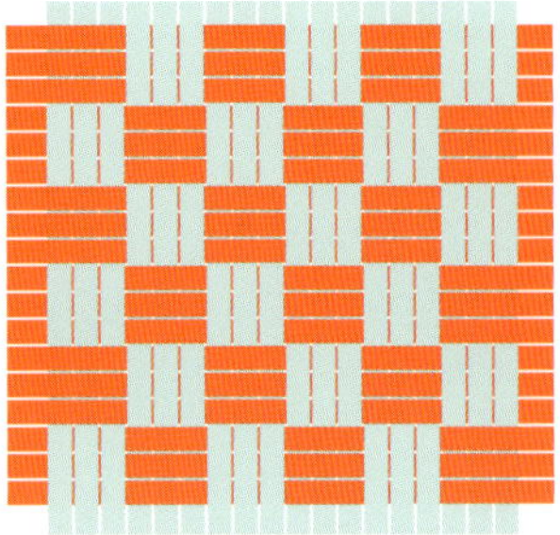

20 Pass the needle under some of the wrapped threads on the back and pull the needle through.

21 Make some loops to secure the thread and trim away any excess.

23 Admire your work.

Extras To Try

This structure works with any number of threads; 3/3, 4/4, 5/5, 6/6, as many as you like!

▲ Why not try adding stripes into your hopsack as you go?

▲ Did you know that you can also make a dogtooth using hopsack? Prepare a warp with stripes of 6 dark, 6 light, 6 dark, 6 light threads, then weave the exact same hopsack structure, switching colour every 6 threads.

Project 6

Waffle

This structure creates a three-dimensional pattern, which is where it hails its name from. The 'waffle' structure is also known as 'honeycomb' for reasons that will become obvious once you see the result.

You may recognise this structure from dishcloths or spa dressing gowns. In cotton, the fabric is absorbent, and in wool it makes for a cosy blanket as the small gaps trap and hold pockets of warm air.

You Will Need

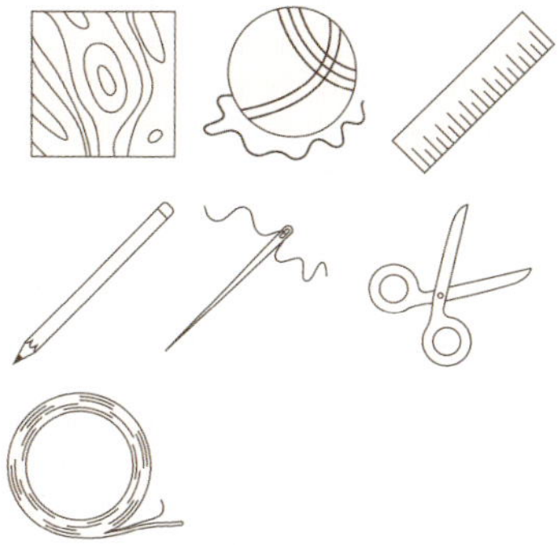

- Base – I used 7 × 7cm (2¾ × 2¾in) for the smaller waffle and 13 × 13cm (5¼ × 5¼in) for the full waffle
- Yarn – I have used chunky rug wool and 4-ply wool
- Ruler
- Pencil
- Flat bodkin needle or a regular sharp one
- Scissors
- Double-sided adhesive tape

Tip While you can use yarn of any thickness, if you are using multiple colours they should all be of the *same* thickness.

Structure

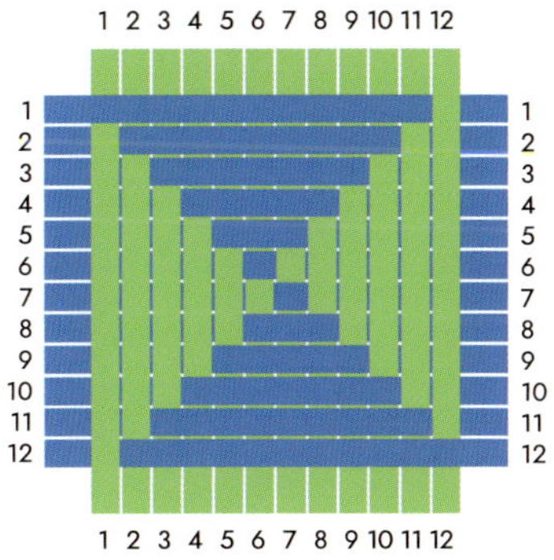

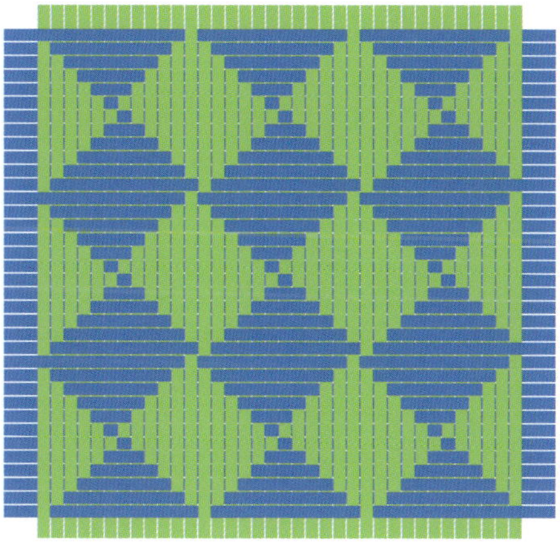

- There are 12 warp threads and 12 weft threads in each repeat of the pattern.
- This structure is versatile. Depending on how many colours you use and where you place them, a whole host of striking patterns can be achieved (see pages 160–61 for design options).
- The waffle is a very different structure to the twill or hopsack with very different results.
- First, I will demonstrate weaving one single repeat of the pattern using a chunky rug wool so that you can see exactly what's going on, then we'll design our colours and create a larger piece using a 4-ply yarn.

Steps

1 Add a couple of strips of tape to the back, then peel them away.

2 Begin to wrap your warp – just 12 threads this time.

3 Cut the end and tuck it under on the back.

4 Here's the warp, ready to go. Cut a length of weft thread in a contrasting colour, and attach it on the back.

Weft 1

5 Pass the needle under 1 warp thread, and over the remaining 11.

6 Wrap the thread around the back after each row.

Weft 2

7 Pass the needle under 2, over 9 and under 1.

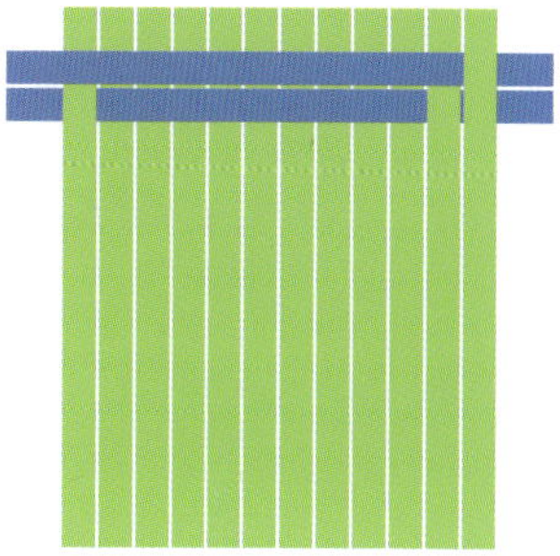

Weft 3

8 Pass the needle under 3, then over 7 and under 2.

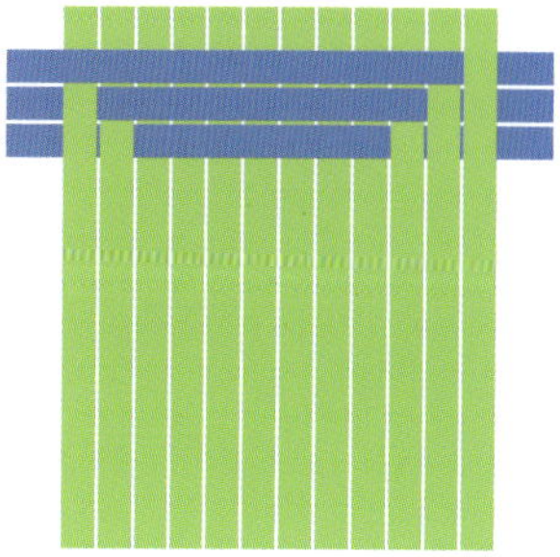

Weft 4

9 Pass the needle under 4, then over 5 and under 3.

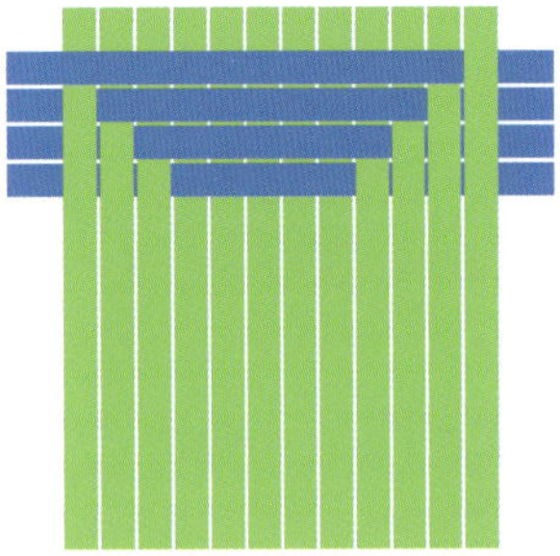

Weft 5

10 Pass the needle under 5, then over 3 and under 4.

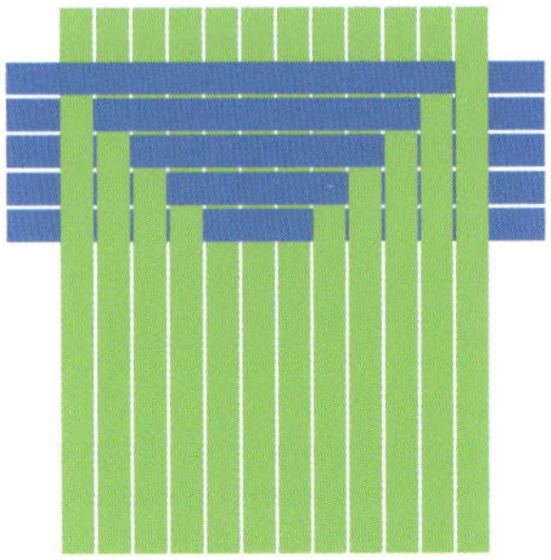

Weft 6

11 Pass the needle under 6, then over 1 and under 5.

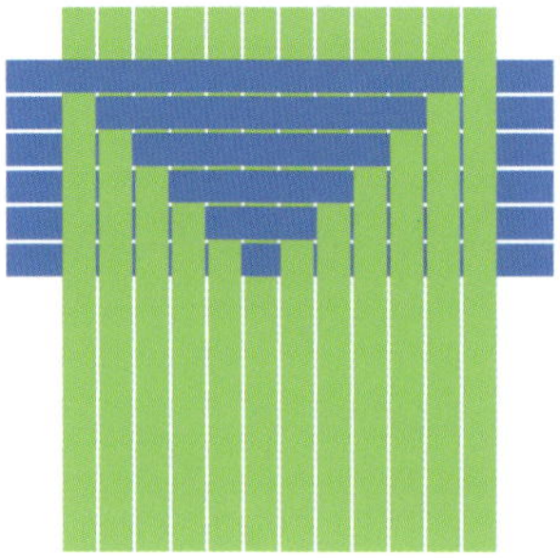

Weft 7

12 Pass the needle under 5, then over 1 and under 6.

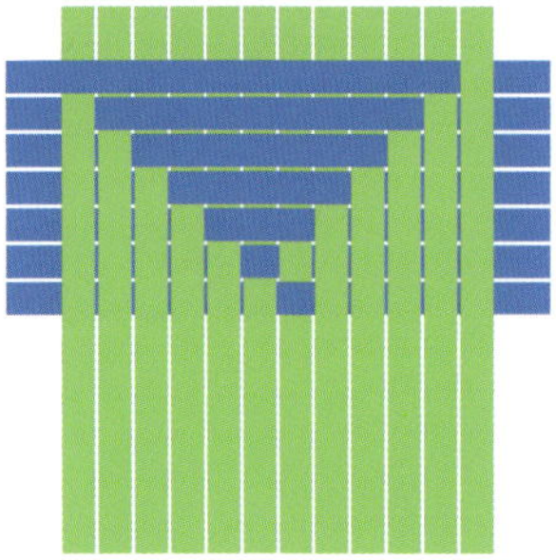

Tip Take care with Weft 7 as it's easy to make a mistake. Remember that you are going over the single thread **directly to the right** of the one from the previous row.

Weft 8

13 Pass the needle under 4, then over 3 and under 5.

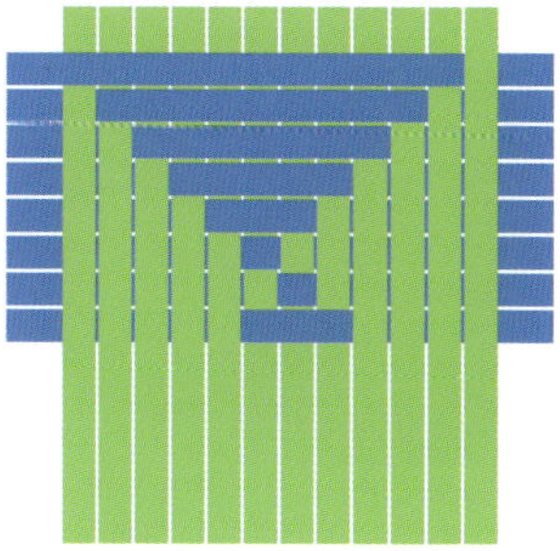

Weft 9

14 Pass the needle under 3, then over 5 and under 4.

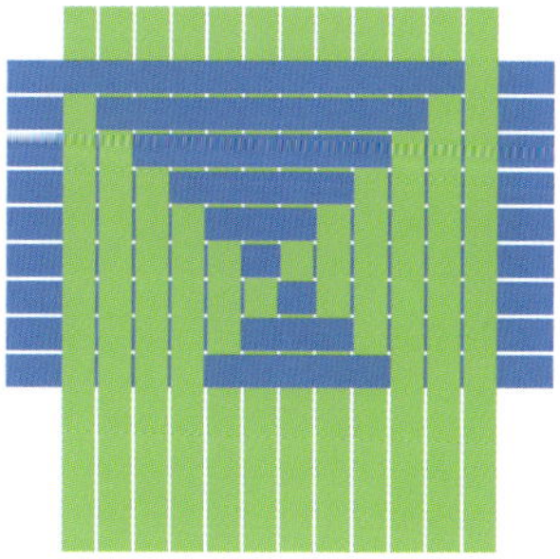

Weft 10

15 Pass the needle under 2, then over 7 and under 3.

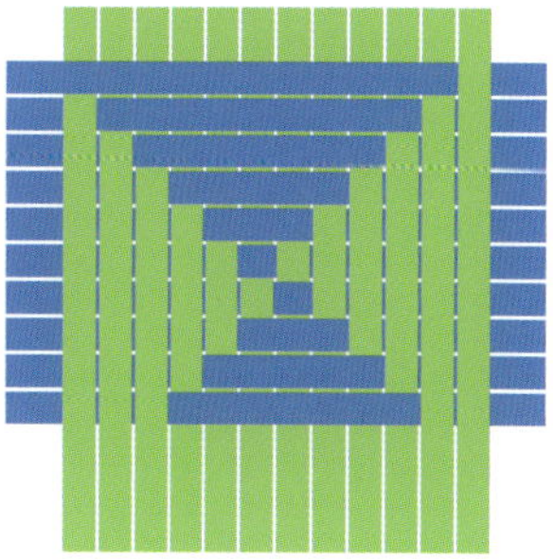

Weft 11

16 Pass the needle under 1, then over 9 and under 2.

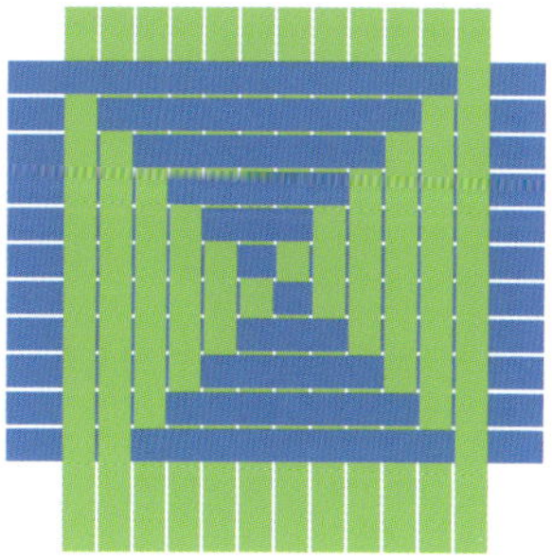

Weft 12

17 Pass the needle over 11 and then under 1.

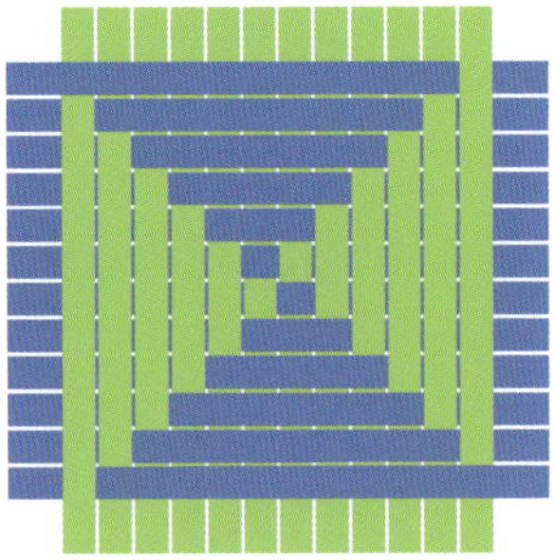

18 Done! Secure the end of the thread on the back.

Full Waffle: Steps

Now we'll put the single waffle pattern into repeat and weave a full waffle on a larger base. See pages 160–61 for some stripe design options. I'll be demonstrating a four-colour option, with two colours in the warp and two in the weft.

Single repeat

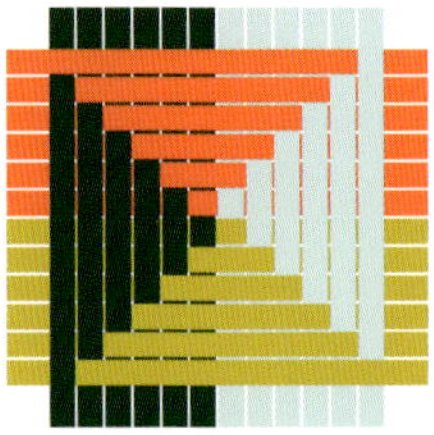

Two repeats each way

Three repeats each way

1 I have wrapped 6 dark green, 6 light green, 6 dark green, 6 light green all the way across.

2 Another way of wrapping stripes is to wrap all of one colour first, leaving gaps for the other colour. This saves on all the knot tying. Now fill in the gaps with your second colour, securing the ends in the usual way.

3 Choose two colours for your wefts. Measure out your thread by wrapping 6 times around the board. Attach the end of the thread to the back of the board.

Weft 1

4 Begin with under 1, then over 11. Repeat all the way across. Remember, each repeat consists of 12 threads.

Tip You will notice that you can **use the stripes as a reference point**, a guide to ensure you are picking up the same sequence of threads with each repeat.

Weft 2

5 Begin with **under 2 at the edge**, then over 9, under 3, over 9, under 3 and so on, until you end the row with under 1.

Weft 3

6 Weft 3 begins with **under 3 at the edge**, then over 7, under 5, over 7, under 5 and so on, until you end the row with under 2.

Weft 4

7 Begin with **under 4 at the edge**, then over 5, under 7, over 5, under 7 and so on, until you end the row with under 3.

Weft 5

8 Begin with **under 5 at the edge**, then over 3, under 9, over 3, under 9 and so on, until you end the row with under 4.

Weft 6

9 Begin with **under 6 at the edge**, then over 1, under 11, over 1, under 11, ending the row with under 5.

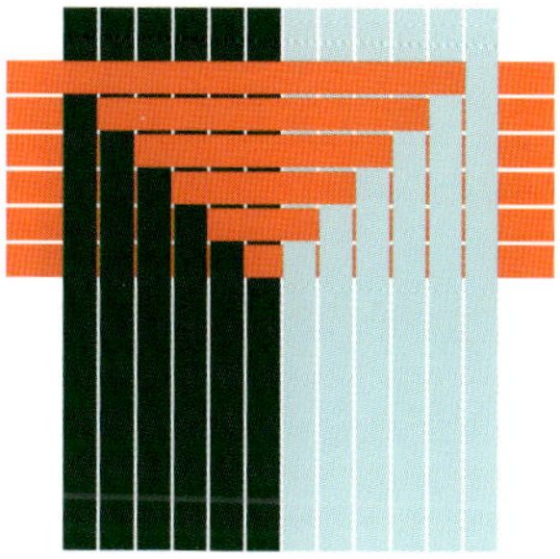

10 Now that you have woven six of your wefts (half of the repeat), it's time to change to another colour. Tie a knot to attach the end of the new thread to the end of the old thread, making sure the knot falls on the back and not the front of the board.

Weft 7

11 Begin with **under 5 at the edge**, then over 1, under 11, over 1, under 11, over 1, under 11 and so on, until you end the row with under 6. The single thread that you go over will be **exactly one thread to the right** of the one in the previous row.

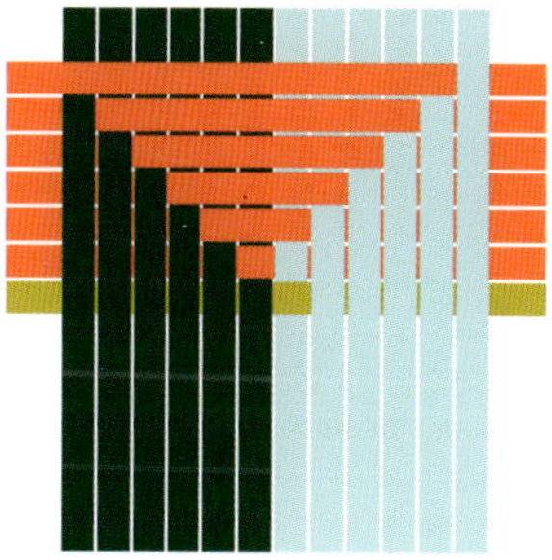

Weft 8

12 Begin with **under 4 at the edge**, then over 3, under 9, over 3, under 9, over 3, under 9 and so on, until you end the row with under 5.

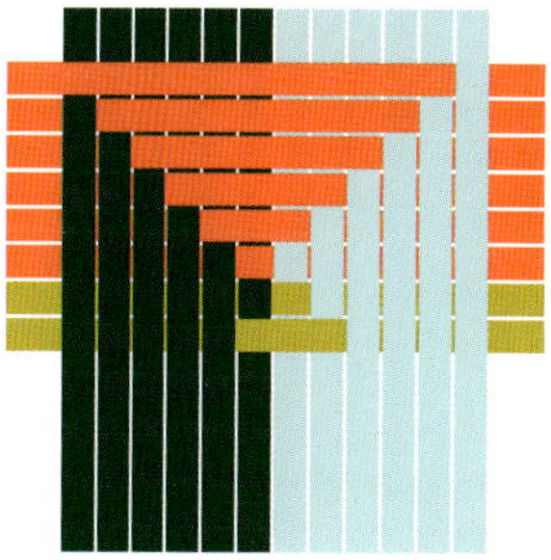

Weft 9

13 Begin with **under 3 at the edge**, then over 5, under 7, over 5, under 7, over 5, under 7 and so on, until you end the row with under 4.

Weft 10

14 Begin with **under 2 at the edge**, then over 7, under 5, over 7, under 5, over 7, under 5 and so on, until you end the row with under 3.

Weft 11

15 Begin with **under 1 at the edge**, then over 9, under 3, over 9, under 3, over 9, under 3 and so on, until you end the row with under 2.

Weft 12

16 Begin with **over 11, then under 1**. This repeats the same over and over again across the warp.

17 That's one whole sequence complete – now do it all again. Tie your first colour on again, ready to repeat the first six wefts.

18 Begin the next repeat exactly the same way as you began the first, starting with Weft 1.

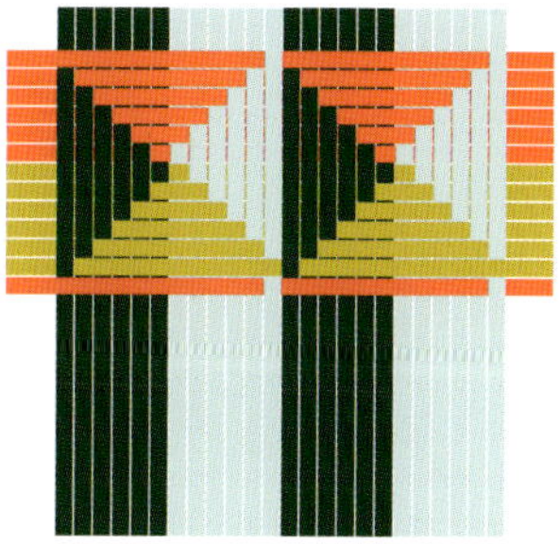

19 This is what two full repeats looks like. Keep going.

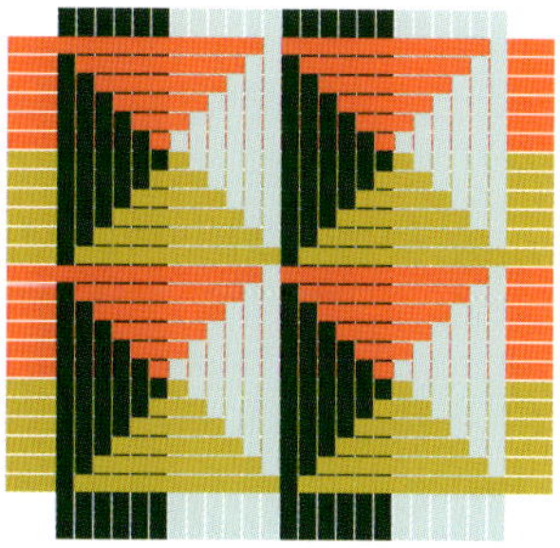

20 Here's three repeats...

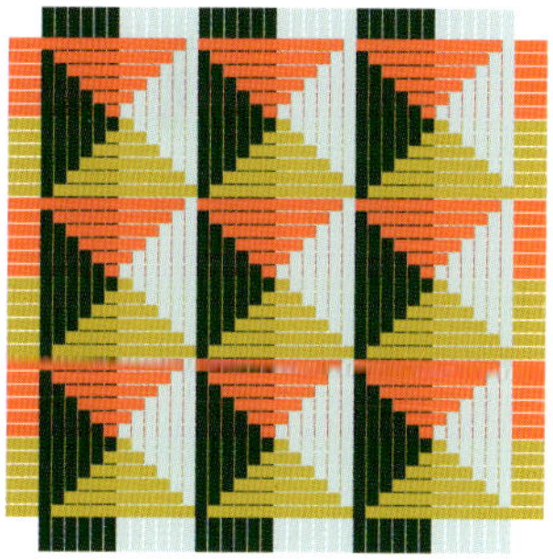

21 When you've finished, secure the end on the back. Trim away any excess thread. This is what the finished piece looks like.

▲ Why not try adding a border of twill around your waffle?

Waffle Options

Here are some examples of the many patterns that can be achieved just by changing colours and stripe placements in the warp and the weft. Remember, the structure is exactly the same in all of these.

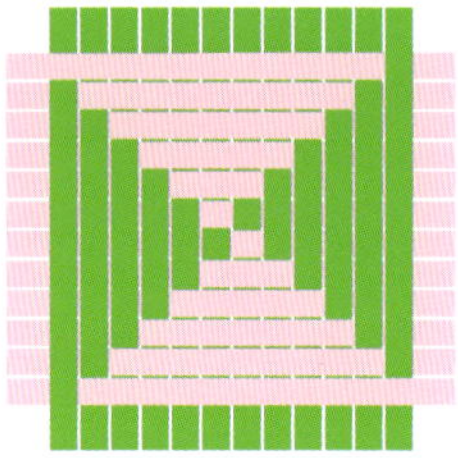

▲ **Diamonds:** one colour warp, one colour weft.

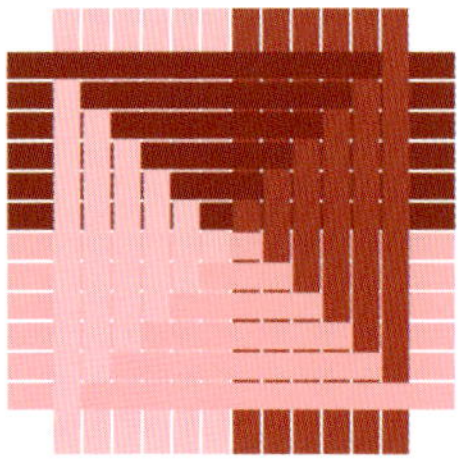

▲ **Two colours:** stripes of six.

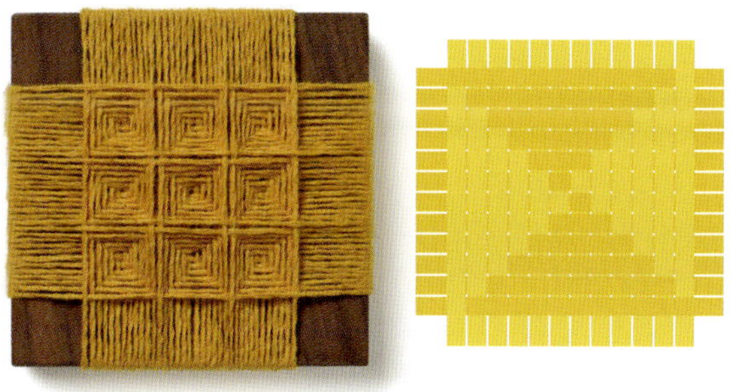

▲ **Solid colour.**

▲ **Super 3D:** three colours, stripes of four.

▲ **Four colours:** two in the warp, two in the weft. Tonal from dark to light.

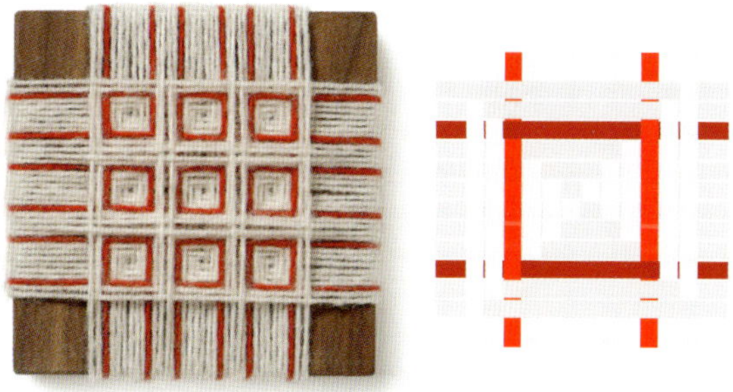

▲ **Red box outline:** each repeat has 2 light, 1 dark, 6 light, 1 dark, 2 light.

▲ **Blue box:** each repeat has 3 light, 6 dark, 3 light.

▲ **Spirals:** 1 black, 1 white, 1 black, 1 white in both warp and weft.

Chapter 14

Rock Weaving

I first started weaving around things in the 2020 lockdown. Cardboard at first, then coasters, old notebooks, things I could find around the house. Discovering that it was quite addictive, I soon moved on to things I could find outside: rocks, slate, driftwood, found objects, broken tiles. I realised the scope of items I could weave around – anything that could support threads being wrapped both ways.

During lockdown, local communities started doing little things to stay connected. One of these was leaving little painted stones in the village – on walls, tops of post boxes, steps and windowsills. On one of our daily walks we saw a long, winding line of painted stones, forming the shape of a snake. One person had started it, by painting the snake's face on a larger stone, and slowly more rocks were added by others to form the body. The colourful stones featured messages of positivity and pictures of hopeful things. It created excitement and joy and kept people connected, despite being physically apart.

During the writing of this book we spent a month up north. I was there to write, but the landscape was so inspiring; there were so many great rocks, and luckily I had brought a bag of threads just in case. While we were there we noticed a little knitted heart hanging from a tree, serving no other purpose than to please passers-by. When we left for home, we decided to leave some woven rocks here and there, as a small offering of thanks to the land and community that made us feel so welcome.

A woven rock feels to me like a supportive hug, the threads wrapped like arms around the rock. They represent our connection to nature and reflect a very human (and animal) instinct to build structures.

Finding Good Rocks

Don't be afraid of odd or irregular-shaped rocks – even jagged and slanted ones can be woven around in one way or another. Some shapes and surfaces are more challenging than others, so here's a guide:

▲ A square or rectangular rock will always be the easiest to weave around, but any rock with four straight-ish edges will work.

▲ Rocks with rounded edges can work. Be careful not to wrap too close to the curve as threads can slip off.

▲ Slightly odd-shaped rocks can often accommodate a warp somewhere.

▲ Sloped edges can be tricky but can work well if they're not too smooth. If one of the four sides is sloped, the threads can tend to slide down to the narrowest bit, but if there is some texture to the surface, threads can be better held in place.

Rock Weaving Examples

Here are some of the rock weavings created by participants of my classes. See how they have allowed the rocks to decide how the weave sits on them? Allowing the rock shape to dictate the result teaches us to let go of perfection – an excellent life mantra.

▲ *Weaving on Grey Slate*, Lynne Francis, 2023

▲ *Rock I* and *Rock II*, Christine Sweeney, 2024

▲ *Weavings on Rock and Glass*, Anne Bochsler, 2023

▲ *Moxie*, Kate Bolton, 2025

Project 7

Rock Weaving

Structure

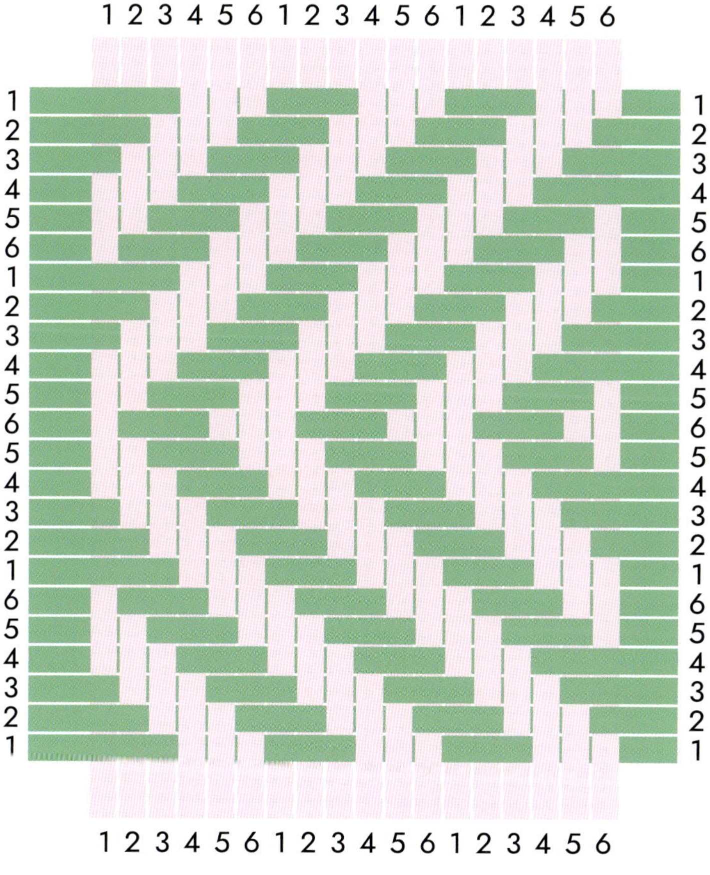

Although a twill is used here, any of the structures shown in this book can be used to weave around a rock, including waffle, hopsack, checks, dogtooth and mini patterns!

You Will Need

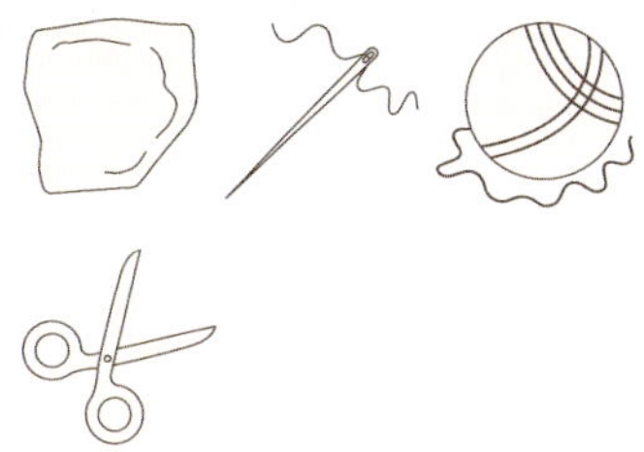

- A rock to weave around
- Flat bodkin or regular sharp needle
- Yarn – anything will do; I am using 6-ply cotton embroidery floss
- Scissors

Steps

1 Double-sided tape doesn't stick well to most rock surfaces, so you'll wrap your warp without it. Hold the end down with your thumb and begin to wrap, in the same way as when using a wooden base. As you wrap, overlap the diagonal end to hold it in place. Once you've wrapped a few times, the end will be securely trapped and you can take your thumb off.

2 If you are weaving on both sides, check the other side often to make sure the threads are all straight. Keep wrapping until you are happy with your warp.

Tip Remember, you don't have to centralise your weaving on the rock, and you don't have to cover the whole thing. I would aim for at least 6 warp threads to get the full benefit of the patterns.

3 Cut the thread, leaving enough length to thread your needle, then pass the thread under all the other warp threads. If you are weaving on both sides, it doesn't matter which side you do this on.

4 Use the needle to tuck the end under the other wrapped threads. Pull the thread through.

5 Trim any remaining thread away. Leave small tails in case you need to pull to tighten them at any point during the weaving process. Don't worry – all tails will be hidden at the end. If you are only weaving on one side, you can use the looping technique on the back.

6 Now you are ready to weave your rock. Cut a length of weft thread, and thread the needle. Attach the thread by passing it under all the wrapped threads on one side of the rock. If you are weaving only on one side, do this on the back. Pull the thread through but leave a small tail.

Weft 1

7 Turn the rock over, and weave your first row. Under 3, then over 3, then under 3, then over 3, all the way across. Pull the thread through.

8 If you are weaving on both sides, turn the rock over and repeat this row in exactly the same way. If you are weaving only on one side, simply wrap the thread around the back. Bring it back around to the front, ready to begin your second row.

9 Pull the weft through and carefully wrap the thread over the original diagonal end, securing it in place.

Weft 2

10 On the front, begin to weave your second row. Over 1 at the edge, then back to over 3 and under 3, over 3 and under 3 all the way across. Compact the wefts using the needle.

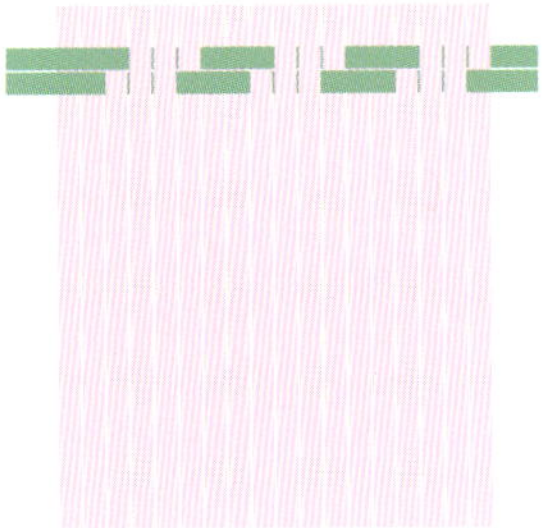

11 Weave the same row on the other side of the rock. Now compact the wefts on this side.

Weft 3

12 Begin with over 2 at the edge, then under 3, over 3, under 3, over 3 and so on.

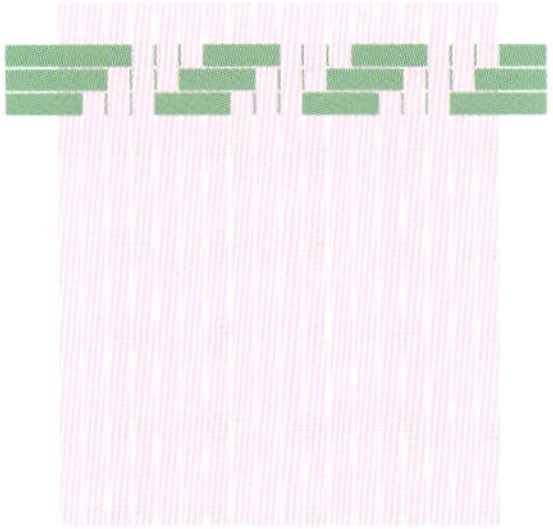

13 Repeat on the other side.

Weft 4

14 Begin with over 3 at the edge, then under 3, over 3, under 3, over 3, all the way across.

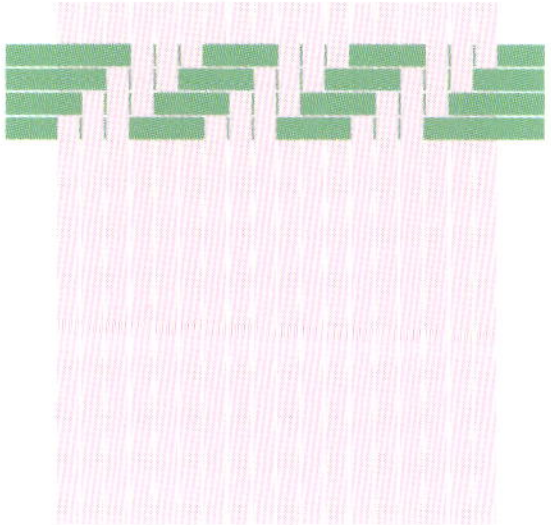

15 Repeat on the other side.

Weft 5

16 Begin with under 1, then back to over 3, under 3, over 3, under 3.

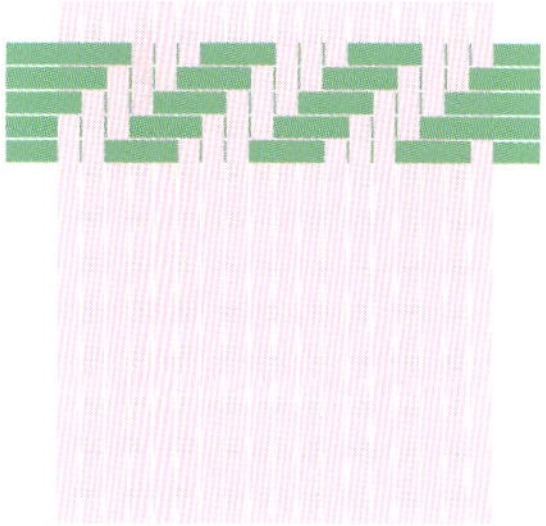

17 Repeat on the other side or wrap around the back.

Weft 6

18 Begin with under 2, then back to over 3, under 3, over 3, under 3.

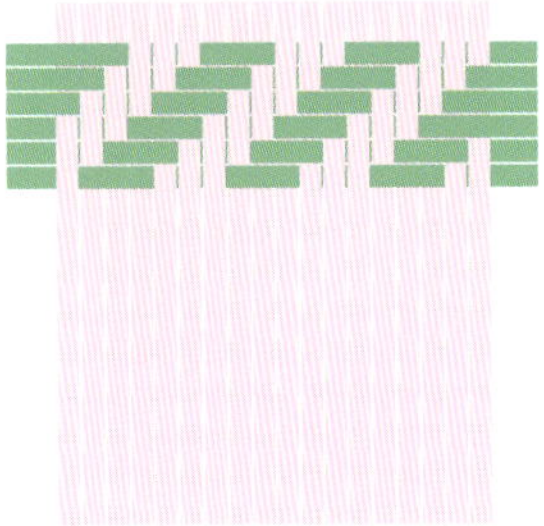

19 Repeat on the other side.

20 When you run out of thread, pass the needle diagonally under the weaving and pull the thread through.

21 Trim the end, leaving a tail in the top corner. This can be hidden later.

22 Attach a new length of thread by passing the needle diagonally downwards under the weaving on the other side. Pull the thread through, leaving a small tail.

23 Begin the sequence again, starting from weft 1.

24 Keep weaving until you feel you've come to a natural place to stop.

25 If you want to, you can weave a different pattern on each side. Why not try a zigzag or a hopsack?

26 Secure the end of the thread. To finish, turn the rock over and pass the needle diagonally under the woven area. Pull the thread through, leaving a small tail.

27 Snip the tails away. To secure the end of the thread, turn the rock over and pass the needle diagonally under the woven area. Pull the thread through, leaving a small tail.

28 If you have only woven on one side, the looping technique can be used to secure the last thread on the back.

Chapter 15

Yarn Wrapping

The following yarn wrapping techniques are a wonderful precursor to off-loom weaving. If you'd like to dip your feet with something a little simpler before taking the plunge with 'proper' woven structure, these projects are a fun and accessible alternative!

Though simpler and often quicker to do, yarn wrappings can have just as big an impact aesthetically as any of the more complex designs in this book.

Use these projects to explore a colour palette, design a stripe, or play with shapes and composition. Make bunting, signage, artwork to be framed for the wall, or a gift for a friend. Most of all, have fun making it up as you go. There are no simulations to follow here, only gentle guidance and a lot of artistic licence!

Project 8

Yarn Wrapping 'Make It Up As You Go!'

The beauty of this technique is that you don't have to follow any specific woven structure, which eliminates the pressure of 'getting it right'. This is intuitive in terms of both thread placement and colour. This time, you'll be weaving your threads over and under wherever you want, in totally random places.

You Will Need

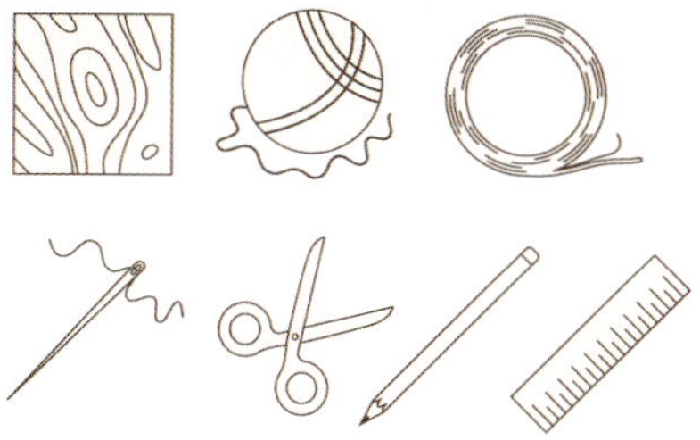

- Base – mine is 15 × 21cm (6 × 8¼in)
- Yarn – I have used a variety of shiny cotton embroidery floss, approximately 6–8 ply
- Double-sided adhesive tape
- Flat bodkin or regular sharp needle
- Scissors
- Pencil
- Ruler

Steps

1 If you want to, mark out your start and finish lines and lay some strips of double-sided tape on the back. Peel a couple of backing strips away. Choose your first colour and begin to wrap your stripes.

2 If you didn't use tape, once the end has been trapped in place, it will be safe to let go.

3 Tie a knot to change colour and continue wrapping your stripes. Peel off the backing strips as you go.

4 Keep going until you are happy with your stripe, and you've reached the finish line.

5 Turn the board over and pass the needle under a few wrapped threads. Pull the needle through. Make some loops to secure the thread.

6 Choose a weft colour to begin with. Attach the end of the thread to the back of the board using the looping technique.

7 Turn the board over so that you are looking at the front, and begin weaving over and under wherever you want. You don't have to go over and under between colours, you can weave into the middle of a section of colour to make it extra interesting.

8 Continue weaving over and under wherever you like. It doesn't matter whether you end on an over or an under.

9 Once you've woven your first row, pull the remaining thread through and wrap the thread around the back, ready to begin the next row. Repeat the exact same row over and over again.

10 When you run out of thread, just tie a knot to attach more. Keep going until you are ready to change colour.

11 Tie a knot to change colour.

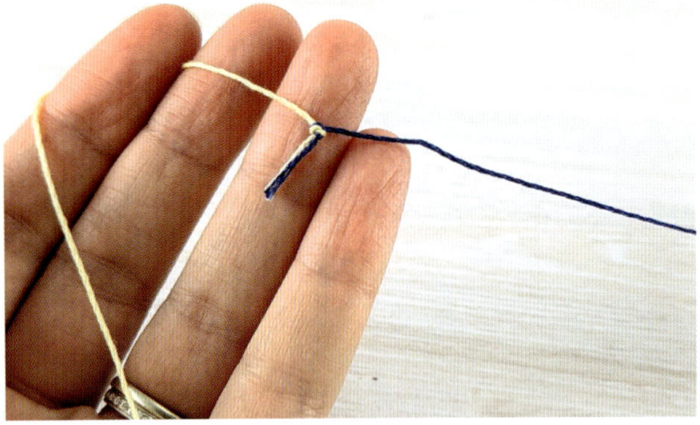

12 This time, choose different places to go over and under. Try to make them quite irregular so that they are not matching in any way to the previous section.

Tip You can leave a gap between sections or weave right up to the previous colour. There are no rules.

13 Play around with the scale of each stripe – even the thinnest stripes can have a big impact.

14 On to the next colour – try to cover different parts of the warp with each section. Keep adding more sections in different colours, taking a step back now and then to judge colour balance.

Tip I tend to weave quite large areas at once to achieve distinct blocks of colour.

15 This time, I've left a gap between sections, and tried a set of stripes alternating two colours.

16 Keep adding more sections, as randomly placed as possible, until you reach the end. Secure the thread on the back.

Extras To Try

▲ Try using just two colours in a stripe going both ways. Here I've stuck to 2 white, 2 blue all the way through, but kept the weft placement random and the sections quite blocky.

Project 9

Yarn Wrapping 'Over and Under'

This one is a great bridge between yarn wrapping and proper weaving. This technique is well suited to thinner threads but any thread thickness will work. I have used a different colour for each stripe – see more design options on page 190.

You Will Need

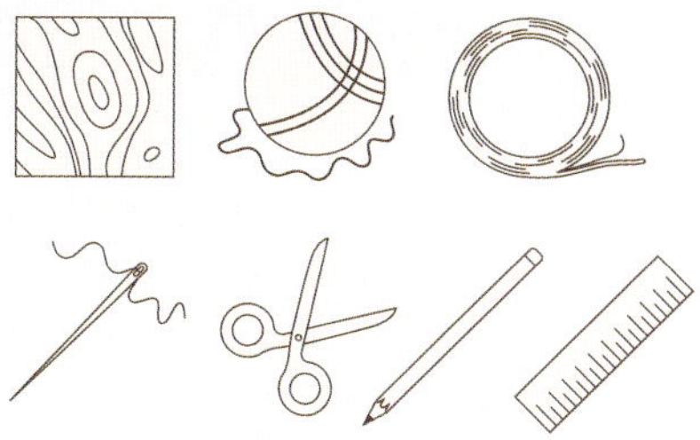

- Square or rectangle base – mine is 12 × 12cm (4¾ × 4¾in)
- Yarn – I am using thin, shiny cotton sewing threads
- Double-sided adhesive tape
- Regular sharp needle
- Scissors
- Pencil
- Ruler

Steps

1 This time, when you wrap your warp stripes, leave a small gap between them. It can be helpful to mark out your stripes (and the gaps between) on the back of the board using a pencil and ruler. My stripes are approx. 1.6cm (⅝in) wide, with a gap of 5mm (¼in) between them. I've left about 2cm (¾in) free in the corners.

2 Apply tape just within the areas that will be covered with yarn (not in the gaps). Peel away the first backing strip only.

3 Begin to wrap your first colour. Remember to wrap over the end of the thread to help secure it in place. Stop when you reach the next marker. Now it's time to change colour.

4 Keep wrapping until you reach the marker, then tie on your next colour.

5 Begin wrapping your second colour within your marked-out space, making sure to leave a gap in between.

6 Complete your second stripe, then your third and fourth stripes.

7 Pass the needle under some of the wrapped threads on the back. Pull the needle through.

8 Loop the thread around a couple of times to secure it and trim away any excess thread.

9 Choose your first weft colour, cut a length and attach one end to the back using the looping technique. Now you are ready to weave.

Stripe 1

10 Pass the needle **over** the whole first stripe, and **under** the whole second stripe. Pull the thread through.

11 Go **over** the whole third stripe, and **under** the whole fourth stripe.

12 This is how your first row will look. Wrap the thread around the back, ready to begin your second weft.

13 Repeat the exact same overs and unders until you have completed your whole first stripe.

Stripe 2

14 Tie your second colour to the end of your first colour so that the knot will appear on the back. This time, you are passing the needle under the first stripe and over the second.

15 Then under the third stripe, and over the fourth (the exact opposite to the last section).

17 Once you've repeated that again and again, your stripe will look like this.

Stripe 3

18 Choose another colour and begin the process again. **Over** the first stripe, **under** the second (opposite again to the previous section).

19 Repeat the same row until your third stripe section is complete.

Stripe 4

20 Finally, choose another colour and switch your overs and unders again. This is how your last row will look.

21 Repeat the same row until the stripe is complete. Finish by securing the final thread on the back of the board using the looping technique. Trim away any excess thread. Done!

Extras To Try

▲ Using two colours, alternate each stripe in both warp and weft.

▲ Using narrower stripes in groups of threes.

Project 10

Yarn Wrapping 'Grid Plait'

For this design, I have used thick card (matboard or mountboard), which is a little lighter weight than wood, making it more suitable for greetings cards. The technique is well suited to thinner threads, especially if you'd like to mount the artwork onto a card base.

You Will Need

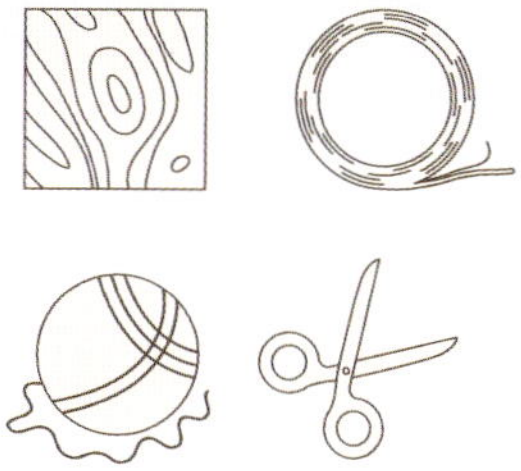

- Base – mine is 1.5mm (0.6in/1500 microns) mountboard cut to 9 × 11cm (3½ × 4⅜in)
- Double-sided adhesive tape
- Yarn – I am using thin, shiny cotton sewing threads
- Scissors

Steps

1 Lay tape all over the back of your card, up to the edges, and press down firmly.

2 This time, remove *all* the backing strips in one go. You will be wrapping both ways so you need the whole back side to be sticky all the way through the process.

3 Choose your first colour, and stick the end down diagonally towards the corner you will begin wrapping from.

4 Wrap a few times (I did about seven wraps) and then leave a small gap. Wrap another stripe of the same number of threads next to the first.

5 You can decide how many stripes to wrap in one go – I've gone for three this time. Cut and lay the end of the thread down onto the sticky tape. Here's how your first stripes might look.

6 Choose another colour, turn the board and start wrapping widthways. Begin quite close to the edge. Wrap any number of stripes; 1, 2, 3 or, like I have, 4.

7 Choose another colour, turn the board and wrap longways again, next to your other stripes.

Tip Switch up the number of stripes you wrap each time to add a little randomness and allow the colours and proportions to interact.

8 Turn the board again, and wrap some stripes widthways in another colour.

9 Turn the board again and change colour again. Keep building your stripes each way. As you add more you will notice the ways the colours interact, with some areas covered and others not.

10 You might like to use a bright statement colour in small doses to make it pop against the other hues.

11 As you near the finish, the space remaining will determine how many stripes you can fit going each way.

12 Just about enough room for two more stripes widthways... and time to choose the final colour for the last stripe.

13 Find somewhere to lay the final end on the back of the board – you may need to add a little more tape to do this. Trim away any excess threads.

14 If you'd like to mount your artwork to a folded card base, cover the back in some strips of double-sided tape.

Extras To Try

▲ Choosing card bases in alternative colours can bring out your designs. Try playing with proportions, colour, wrapping order, leaving empty space, or covering every bit of white.

Project 11

Yarn Wrapping 'Letter'

These look great not only framed as singular letters but also for spelling out names or words, strung together as bunting. While a square base can work, I find that rectangles allow more space for 'taller' letters.

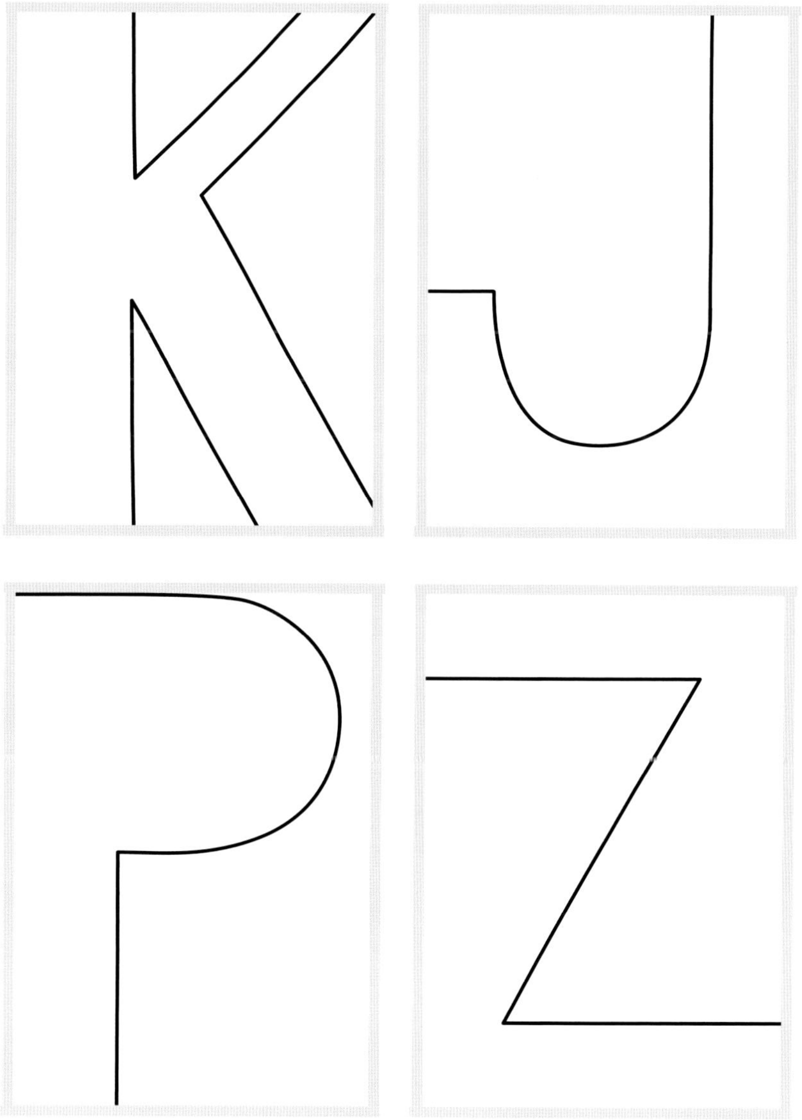

You Will Need

- Square or rectangular base – mine is A6, postcard sized
- Yarn – I'm using 6-ply shiny cotton embroidery floss
- Card for making a template
- Pen
- Needle – a flat bodkin needle is great for this, though a regular sharp needle comes in handy towards the end as things become tighter
- Scissors
- Double-sided adhesive tape

You can download the full A–Z at printable size here:

Steps

1 Cover the whole back side with tape. Peel off the tape on the side on which you'll start weaving.

2 Start wrapping your warp almost from the edge of the board – leave 1mm to stop the threads from falling off the sides.

Tip Choose a light colour for your warp, as you will be drawing the letter shape directly onto it.

3 Wrap all the way across, stopping 1mm from the edge.

4 Cut the thread, leaving enough length to thread your needle. Pass the end under some of the wrapped threads on the back, and pull it through.

5 Make some loops to secure the thread in place and trim away any excess yarn.

6 Take a piece of card and draw around the base to make a letter stencil.

7 Make some allowance at the edges to ensure your letter has a little space around it.

8 Draw your letter. Adding 'holes' to the letter also works well – in this example it's a stylistic choice to leave them out. Lowercase letters work well too – sometimes it can be nice to mix them.

9 Cut out your letter shape and position the stencil onto your warp.

10 Carefully draw around the stencil with a pen and think about whether you'd like to fill the letter or the negative space with colour.

Tip Use a biro rather than an inky pen to avoid ink running down the threads.

11 Prepare some weft thread in a contrasting colour and attach the weft on the back, quite close to the top of the board.

12 I've chosen to fill the negative space with colour. Simply wrap the top part until you reach the start of the letter shape.

13 On your next row, find the ink spot and pass your needle under from that point. Try to cover the inky thread. Pull the thread through and push the row up to join the others.

14 Find the next inky spot, passing the needle over the ink and under the rest of the following threads. Pull the thread through. Push this row up to join the others.

15 Find the next ink spot and do the same again. Pull the thread through and push this row up.

16 Keep doing the same, following the pen line as you go. When you run out of thread, just knot a new piece on.

17 Keep going, following the curve – sometimes you just move one thread over, sometimes two, sometimes you repeat the same row twice. Now we're halfway!

Tip Not all letters are rounded – some have straight lines like 'L', 'E' or 'F', others have diagonals like 'A' or 'V'. Each letter presents a new learning curve.

18 The last part will simply be wrapped, like the start. Done!

19 Secure the end of the thread on the back of the board. Pull the needle through and trim away any excess.

Extras To Try

You can find a booklet of pre-made A-Z alphabet shapes online (see page 199). These are best printed onto card, if possible. Each letter stencil is A6 to fit the wooden base size used in the project.

▲ Try weaving into the wrapped threads – either just one way or both ways. This time, instead of wrapping threads around the back, just weave back and forth on the front of the board. Be careful not to allow the edges to pull in too much. Due to the back and forth of the wefts, a little improvisation will be required at the selvedges, but this is a great opportunity to try out the good old 'make it up as you go' approach, passing the needle over and under wherever you like. No need to follow a pattern – just intuition and a bit of artistic licence.

▲ Lowercase letters look great too and can be a fun aid to teaching the alphabet.

▲ This technique also works well with many shapes besides letters.

Chapter 16

Why Not Try...?

Now that you've had a go at paper weaving, off-loom weaving and yarn wrapping, you may well be brimming with ideas about the many ways you can use these new skills! All of the projects in this book can be adapted and reimagined in terms of materials, scale, display and use.

Why not try weaving around a three-dimensional base? What happens if you cut shapes out of your paper weavings? What if you work into your weavings and merge your new skills with other craft techniques such as collage, sculpture, stitch, ceramics or embroidery?

▶ Twill, waffle, plait and 'make it up as you go', woven on 5 × 5cm (2 × 2in) wooden pieces.

Festive Decorations

Wooden Baubles

These gorgeous hanging decorations needn't be limited to sparkly threads – colour works fabulously too. Their small scale makes them fairly quick – a perfect crafting project in the run up to the festive period – and they make lovely gifts too.

Simulations for two styles (Plait and Steps) are below. Why not try a mix of yarns and stripes of colour – checks look great too!

1 Drill a small hole in one corner before you start wrapping threads.

◀ 'Steps' for tree decoration.

2 Simply thread a length of yarn through the hole to make a loop for hanging.

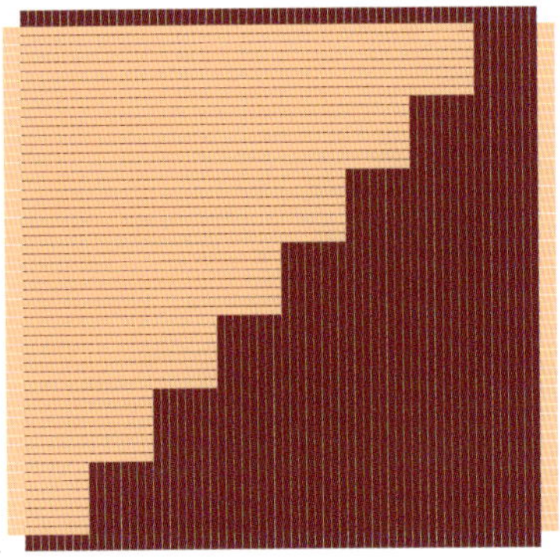

◀ 'Plait' for tree decoration.

Paper-weaving Shapes

To cut shapes out of your paper weavings, draw a stencil on the back, and then cover the entire back with tape to secure the weave. If you want to make a bauble to hang on the tree, cut out two circles and use double-sided tape to stick them together, sandwiching a loop of thread in between.

Woven Picture Frames

These simple frames work so well for messages of love and affirmations – but the weaving can also be used to 'trap' artworks and photos. Instead of weaving in the centre of the wood and leaving the corners free, try weaving in the corners and leaving the centre free. It can be fun to match the colours of the weaving to those in the artwork. They can be simple yarn wrappings, or woven patterns like twill, dogtooth or even a waffle in each corner.

Tip Make sure the yarn does not slip off the corners. A little double-sided tape on the back in the corners helps, as does leaving a 1mm space rather than wrapping right up to the edges.

Making It Up

It can be fun to throw instructions and simulations to the side, and just... make up your own. Here, I've banned counting threads, opting to pass the needle over and under wherever I please. As this is an artwork rather than a practical fabric, we don't need to worry about its stability as a cloth. No need for straight edges and no such thing as mistakes here – all you need is the joy of colour and thread.

Framing Your Work

There are many different ways to display your woven pieces – framing is just one. Often, our unframed pieces remain in our studios, in boxes, in piles or in sketchbooks – but framing can transform a piece from a private experiment into something shared and celebrated. Whether it's a singular artwork, a pair or a set of multiples, framing your pieces elevates them and helps them to feel properly finished.

Most framers will offer a variety of colours and finishes for the outer frames themselves, as well as the mounting boards inside the frame. This can be great if you think you'd like to match the frame to

Tip If you're framing something heavy like a rock, you may need a super-strong glue in combination with adhesive pads.

the colours in the weave. A white frame will draw the eye to the piece itself, showing off the details in all their glory, but it can become lost on a white wall. Oak is a great alternative if you'd like to stay minimal or neutral.

I've always found that box frames work well for this type of work because they offer space for an artwork to breathe. If possible, leave plenty of space around the piece to stop it from feeling cramped. I often use adhesive tabs in the corners of the artwork to raise it a little from the surface of the mount board. This gives a lovely floating effect.

Extras To Consider (If Budget Allows)

If photographing your work once it is framed is important to you, I'd recommend opting for non-reflective 'art glass'. Photos will be much easier to take without light distorting the view of your beautiful work. Non-reflective glass is often also UV protected, which helps to protect against fading.

Conservation framing, which involves fully sealing the back, protects against environmental damage such as humidity and insects, but it does mean the frame cannot be opened. Asking for acid-free materials will also help to protect against yellowing.

Chapter 17

An Ode to Unfinishedness

Finishing things can feel great – especially if what we are making is useful, wearable or a gift. It can give us a wonderful sense of accomplishment, of satisfaction and self-reliance. There is nothing better than being asked 'Where did you get that?' and being able to proudly say 'I made it!' However, as you reach the end of this book, you may find yourself with multiple projects in various states of unfinishedness. Welcome to my world. This is a safe space, do come in.

Attitudes to Unfinishedness

I asked my community how they felt about their own unfinished craft projects. It became apparent that while for some finishing is less important compared to the joy of process and practice, many of us only equate 'time well spent' with 'finished' products. For some, finishing is part of the process. The wearing or using of the item becomes part of the experience, attached on to the end of the making process. For others, there is no such thing as 'finished'; its definition blurred, a moving target.

I'd like to introduce the idea of 'unfinishedness' as a friendly and supportive presence in our lives. As someone who mostly enjoys the process of making rather than the completion, I don't always feel motivated to finish a piece. Sometimes I fear that the finished piece will become somehow less beautiful than when it was still in progress. There is something energising about seeing the work halfway through, captured just when the magic has started to happen, the needle still embedded among the threads. Other times I feel sad that a thing is finished. This idea is also explored in *Art and Fear* by David Bayles and Ted Orland as 'a moment of loss – the loss of all the other forms the imagined piece might have taken'.

Many of the crafters I meet tell me that they feel shame about having multiple unfinished projects on the go. They feel they should finish what they are currently working on before starting something new, despite brimming with new ideas during the making process. Some also described the struggle of getting to the end of a piece once the initial excitement of the challenge has faded.

At the beginning, a piece is filled with possibilities, the materials and tools loaded with potential. As we make our way through the work, with every decision, every little progress towards the outcome, our field of possibility narrows.

This sentiment brings to mind the folklore story 'The Old Woman and The Trickster Crow', which goes something like this:

An old woman sits in a cave, weaving her 'tapestry of the world'. Every now and then she pauses to go and stir her soup, gently simmering on the other side of the cave. Each time she leaves the loom, the Trickster Crow flies over and unravels all her hard work, leaving the tapestry in a perpetual state of incompleteness.

Returning to her loom, she begins again, inevitably weaving a slightly different version each time.

She is not attached to one particular outcome. It would be more destructive if she were ever to finish her weaving, as this would signify an end to the story.

Both the 'stirring up' of the soup and the unravelled threads represent possibility; infinite paths to be explored, alternative ways forward.

For me, a 'work in progress' feels much less intimidating than a blank canvas. Often, I'll leave the needle in halfway through a row to make it easier to pick it up and carry on next time. The needle is an invitation to play, a train of thought that is easy to jump back on to. I love to start the day by continuing with an idea that is already established, and I like to start new things before I have finished other things, while an idea is still zingy with inspiration.

Unfinished pieces make excellent teaching examples. The presence of the needle offers clues to how the piece was made, to how long it might have taken. While seeing a finished piece can feel a little intimidating, seeing one part-way through may feel more approachable. To have a go at something, we must first feel inspired and capable. Seeing the process can help with that.

Though we all have projects that are never officially labelled as 'finished', every act of making serves us by stimulating our creativity. There is a valid place for the enjoyment that comes from generating ideas. The sheer number of ideas I have written down in my notes app far outweighs the amount of art I could ever hope to make. The buzz doesn't always stick around for the making part. That's OK. Some ideas are just there to be part of the journey. Nothing is wasted.

What is a finished piece, anyway?

Here's a novel idea. You get to decide when something is finished. If you are what you might conventionally think of as 'halfway through' a piece, you could decide that it is, in fact, finished. You have the freedom and autonomy to make that choice, the piece is yours after all. If you got something positive from the experience of working on it, maybe that is enough. If you feel you have reached the limit of what you can gain from the work, perhaps it is complete as it is. You can decide later that it wasn't finished after all, and continue to work on it.

Maybe the beginning and end points of a piece are not the first and last stitch or brushstroke, but rather the first and last thought or learning that can be drawn from it, which can begin way before the physical making starts and can go on indefinitely afterwards. The making part can just be a vehicle for learning and developing ideas, if you want it to be.

A maker shared with me that she had been working on the same needlework project for thirty-one years. Different parts of the landscape offer different levels of engagement; the sky is repetitive and doesn't require much thought, but the detail in other parts of the imagery present more of a challenge, demanding more focus. Some pieces do not ask to be finished. Some are there to offer us a lifetime of engagement, a few minutes a day.

A Time For Leaving Things Undone

Perhaps there is a time for leaving things undone, and a time for finishing things. For me, this is determined by my energy. Some days I will have a million ideas and start lots of things. Inspiration isn't constant, and I feel I must grab it while it's here, before it slips off again. On the days that my brain feels tired, engaging in simple repetitive movements without too much thought suits me perfectly. Luckily, this is often exactly what is required to finish a piece, and so that is how I will choose to spend my day.

If you feel bad about how many unfinished projects you have on the go, I have excellent news for you. According to Anne Kirketerp, author of *Craft Psychology*, having at least ten projects on the go simultaneously is very healthy indeed and helps us to reach our most inspired and focused state of mind. She comments: 'It is not a sign of indecisiveness or lack of perseverance to have many craft projects on a hobby basis. Both practically and therapeutically, each piece of craft has its time and justification.'

The key is to have a project available to match your energy levels. A simple one for when you're tired, something more complex for when you're feeling like a challenge, and everything in between. This way, however you are feeling you are able to pick something up, and enjoy the benefits of engaging in craft. Similarly, if you run into a problem with one, it is then possible to park it and pick up another until a solution presents itself.

It is OK to come back to things after a long time. Sometimes ideas need more time to develop. Taking a break and returning with fresh eyes is often just what a piece needs. This could be a ten-minute or a ten-year break. When we come back to a project after some time, we might be pleasantly surprised with the quality of the work we left behind, in a way we didn't credit ourselves with at the time. Thoughts of 'Did I really do that?' can give us new confidence in our abilities and motivation to continue the work. As time passes, skills improve, tastes and interests change.

Life is a work in progress. Always learning, always exploring.

Closing Thoughts

◀ First Ever Off-loom Weaving: Cardboard box, hotel sewing kit. Sometimes, good things come from frustration and boredom. Possible uses for this craft are up for interpretation. You are just beginning your journey into this craft. All the joy is ahead of you.

Further Reading

Adams, Sean, *The Designer's Dictionary of Colour*, Abrams, New York, 2017

Albers, Josef, *Interactions of Colour: 50th Anniversary Edition*, Yale University Press, Connecticut, 2013

Bayles, David and Orland, Ted, *Art & Fear: Observations on the Perils (and Rewards) of Artmaking*, Image Continuum Press, Santa Fe, 2001

Danto, Arthur and Joan Simon, *Sheila Hicks: Weaving as Metaphor*, Yale University Press, New Haven, 2006

Fashionary, *Textilepedia: The Complete Fabric Guide*, Fashionary International Ltd, Kowloon, 2020

Hickman, Richard, *Why We Make Art and Why It Is Taught*, University of Chicago Press, Chicago, 2005

Horstman, Fritz, *Interacting with Color: A Practical Guide to Josef Albers's Color Experiments*, Yale University Press, New Haven, 2024

Le Guin, Ursula, *The Carrier Bag Theory Of Fiction*, Ignota, London, 2019

Kary, Nick, *Material*, Chelsea Green Publishing, London, 2024

Kirketerp, Dr Anne, *Craft Psychology: How Crafting Promotes Health*, Mailand, Denmark, 2024

Korn, Peter, *Why We Make Things and Why It Matters: The Education of a Craftsman*, Vintage, New York, 2017

Newport, Cal, *Digital Minimalism*, Penguin Business, London, 2020

Otter, James, *Do/Make: The Power of Your Own Two Hands*, The Do Book Co, London, 2020

Perryman, Laura, *The Colour Bible*, Octopus Publishing, London, 2021

Plato, trans. Benjamin Jowett, *The Statesman*, Oxford University Press, Oxford, 2008

Plato, trans. Benjamin Jowett, *The Laws*, Oxford University Press, Oxford, 2008

Rogowski, Gary, *Handmade: Creative Focus in the Age of Distraction*, Linden Publishing Group, London, 2017

Rubin, Rick, *The Creative Act: A Way of Being*, Canongate Books, Edinburgh, 2025

Sennett, Richard, *The Craftsman*, Yale University Press, Connecticut, 2009

Sowerby, Jessica, *Colour Confidence: A Practical Handbook to Embracing Colour in Your Home*, Quadrille, London, 2023

Wellesley-Smith, Claire, *Resilient Stitch*, Batsford, London, 2021

Acknowledgements

I would like to give special thanks to Stephen Lenthall of Article Studio, for taking such wonderful photographs of the woven pieces, and to Jessica Man for capturing my studio and yarn stash! My thanks also go to Emilia Kalyvides of Design by Emilia for the iconography. And thank you to Andrew Clark at Rewthink and Kate at Another Country for donating so many beautiful wood offcuts.

I am grateful to Clare, Natasha and all the team at Herbert Press for their expertise in compiling this material into such a beautiful book.

I also want to look back to where it all began: a special mention to two very cherished tutors, Berni Yates and Philippa Brock, who provided the foundation for my creative career fifteen years ago. I'd like to acknowledge my online community, and everyone who has ever taken a class with me. Your support has enabled me to continue teaching, creating and doing what I love.

Finally, my thanks to my husband, Chris, for his endless patience and care while I worked on this book, and to my family and friends for being a constant source of encouragement.

Suppliers

Flat Bodkin Needles

UK

John James Needles
jjneedles.com/buy-needles/
needle-threaders-and-bodkins/bodkins

USA and Canada

The Colonial Needle Company
colonialneedle.com/products/cb60700

Italy

Tombolo & Disegni
tombolodisegnishop.it/prodotto/
ago-piatto-per-punto-filza

Yarn

UK

Second-hand Yarn

- **Fairfield Yarns** fairfieldyarns.co.uk
- **Colourmart** colourmart.com
- **The Loom Exchange** theloomexchange.co.uk – a platform for selling and buying second-hand weaving equipment, and occasionally lists yarns.
- **Local guilds or textile craft groups** – a member may be looking to downsize their stash or may know someone that is selling theirs. Guilds often use their meeting halls to host yarn sales or organise studio clearances at members' homes.
- **Charity shops** – a great place to look for second-hand yarn. If you don't see any on the shelves, there may be some in the back – just ask. The Oxfam webshop now has a specific department for 'Sewing, Knitting & Haberdashery'.
- **Second-hand selling platforms** – Gumtree, eBay, Facebook Marketplace, Vinted, Preloved and Etsy can be great resources for second-hand yarn. Remember to check the 'used' box, as a lot of the products listed in these marketplaces are new products masquerading as pre-owned. Avoid listings with multiples of the same product available.

New Yarn

Handweavers Studio & Gallery handweavers.co.uk
Uppingham Yarns wools.co.uk